OSTEOARTHRITIS

PHYSIOTHERAPY ESSENTIALS

NIHAR RANJAN MOHANTY
PRIYABRATA DASH
AMITAV NAYAK
DWARIKANATH ROUT

DEDICATED TO

To all the great teachers of the physiotherapy fraternity across the world,

Your dedication, wisdom, and unwavering commitment inspire generations to heal, grow, and transform lives. This book is a humble tribute to your tireless efforts in shaping the future of our profession and the lives of those we serve.

With deep respect and gratitude.

Nihar Ranjan Mohanty

Priyabrata Dash

Amitav Nayak

Dwarikanath Rout

Contents

Preface

Osteoarthritis (OA) is one of the most prevalent and challenging musculoskeletal conditions, affecting millions worldwide. This book serves as a comprehensive guide to understanding and managing osteoarthritis through the lens of physiotherapy. It integrates the latest evidence-based practices, clinical insights, and practical approaches to help physiotherapists enhance the quality of life for their patients.

From exploring the underlying pathophysiology of OA to detailing individualized treatment plans, this book emphasizes holistic care. It highlights therapeutic exercises, manual therapy, patient education, and the role of technology in rehabilitation.

Designed for students, clinicians, and researchers, this resource aims to bridge the gap between theory and practice, empowering readers to deliver effective and compassionate care to those living with osteoarthritis.

Let this book inspire you to embrace innovation and collaboration in addressing the challenges of OA, ultimately contributing to better patient outcomes.

Acknowledgements

This book is the culmination of countless hours of research, clinical practice, and collaboration. It would not have been possible without the support and encouragement of several individuals and institutions.

First and foremost, we express our heartfelt gratitude to our teachers, whose guidance and expertise have been invaluable throughout this journey. Your insights and constructive feedback have shaped the quality and direction of this work.

We are deeply thankful to our colleagues and peers in the field of physiotherapy, whose discussions and shared knowledge have enriched our understanding of osteoarthritis and its management. Special thanks to Dr Avinash Tiwari (PT), Principal, Sri Jagannath College of Physiotherapy, Nuapada, Odisha for his contributions and support during the writing process.

We would also like to acknowledge the patients whose resilience and determination inspired me to delve deeper into this subject. Your experiences have been a powerful reminder of the impact physiotherapy can have on improving quality of life.

We are immensely grateful to our family and friends for their unwavering support and patience, especially during the demanding phases of this project. Your encouragement kept us motivated and focused.

Finally, we extend our appreciation to KIMS, KIIT Deemed to be University, Bhubaneswar, India for providing the resources and platform to bring this book to fruition.

To all those who played a part in making this book a reality, whether directly or indirectly, we extend our sincere thanks.

With gratitude,
Nihar Ranjan Mohanty
Priyabrata Dash
Amitav Nayak
Dwarikanath Rout

Authors

Nihar Ranjan Mohanty
Associate Professor, KIMS School of Physiotherapy
KIMS, KIIT Deemed to be University, Bhubaneswar, Odisha
Priyabrata Dash
Associate Professor cum Principal (I/C), KIMS School of
Physiotherapy
KIMS, KIIT Deemed to be University, Bhubaneswar, Odisha
Amitav Nayak
Deputy Director, Administration, KIMS School of Physiotherapy
KIMS, KIIT Deemed to be University, Bhubaneswar, Odisha
Dwarikanath Rout
Assistant Professor, KIMS School of Physiotherapy
KIMS, KIIT Deemed to be University, Bhubaneswar, Odisha

CHAPTER I

INTRODUCTION

Osteoarthritis (OA) is a chronic, progressive, and degenerative joint disorder that primarily affects the articular cartilage—the smooth tissue covering the ends of bones in joints. It is the most common form of arthritis and is a leading cause of disability worldwide, especially among older adults. The disease is characterized by joint pain, stiffness, reduced mobility, and structural changes within the joint.

PATHOPHYSIOLOGY

Osteoarthritis involves both mechanical and biological factors that disrupt the balance between the degradation and repair of joint tissues. The disease progresses through the following mechanisms:

1. **Cartilage Breakdown:**

   - The articular cartilage deteriorates due to excessive mechanical stress and altered biochemical processes. This leads to reduced cushioning and increased friction between bones.

2. **Subchondral Bone Changes:**

   - The bone beneath the cartilage, known as the subchondral bone, becomes sclerotic (hardened) and may develop microfractures.

3. **Synovial Inflammation:**

   - Mild inflammation of the synovium (joint lining) occurs, contributing to pain and swelling. Inflammatory mediators like cytokines (e.g., IL-1 and TNF-α) and enzymes (e.g., matrix metalloproteinases) accelerate cartilage degradation.

4. **Osteophyte Formation:**

   - Bone spurs or osteophytes develop at the joint margins as a compensatory response, often leading to joint deformity.

5. **Loss of Joint Space:**

- As cartilage wears away, the space between bones narrows, resulting in friction, pain, and stiffness.

RISK FACTORS

1. **Age:**

- The risk of OA increases with age due to the natural decline in cartilage repair mechanisms.

2. **Genetics:**

- A family history of OA may increase susceptibility.

3. **Obesity:**

- Excess body weight places additional mechanical stress on weight-bearing joints and contributes to systemic inflammation.

4. **Joint Injuries:**

- Previous injuries, such as fractures or ligament tears, can predispose joints to OA.

5. **Repetitive Joint Use:**

- Occupational or recreational activities involving repetitive joint motion increase the risk.

6. **Sex:**

- Women, especially postmenopausal, are more likely to develop OA than men.

CLINICAL FEATURES

- **Pain:**

  - Typically worsens with activity and improves with rest.

- **Stiffness:**

  - Prominent after periods of inactivity, such as morning stiffness lasting less than 30 minutes.

- **Crepitus:**

  - A grating or cracking sound during joint movement.

- **Deformity:**

  - Advanced OA may result in visible joint deformities.

- **Reduced Range of Motion:**

  - Progressive stiffness limits joint flexibility and mobility.

DIAGNOSIS

- **Clinical Evaluation:**

  - Diagnosis is primarily based on patient history, physical examination, and characteristic symptoms.

- **Imaging:**

  - **X-rays:** Reveal joint space narrowing, osteophytes, and subchondral sclerosis.
  - **MRI:** Offers detailed visualization of cartilage and soft tissues, used in atypical cases.

- **Laboratory Tests:**

○ While not diagnostic, blood tests and joint fluid analysis rule out other forms of arthritis, such as rheumatoid arthritis or gout.

MANAGEMENT

The treatment of OA aims to alleviate symptoms, improve joint function, and minimize further joint damage.

1. **Non-Pharmacological:**

   - **Exercise**: Low-impact activities like swimming and cycling strengthen muscles and improve flexibility.
   - **Weight Management**: Reducing body weight decreases stress on joints.
   - **Physical Therapy**: Includes strength training, stretching, and range-of-motion exercises.

2. **Pharmacological:**

   - **Analgesics**: Acetaminophen or nonsteroidal anti-inflammatory drugs (NSAIDs) for pain relief.
   - **Topical Treatments**: Capsaicin or NSAID gels.
   - **Intra-Articular Injections**: Corticosteroids or hyaluronic acid to reduce inflammation and improve lubrication.

3. **Surgical:**

   - Reserved for severe cases where conservative treatments fail.
   - Options include joint replacement (e.g., total knee or hip arthroplasty) or joint realignment procedures.

Physiotherapy Management of Osteoarthritis

Physiotherapy plays a vital role in managing osteoarthritis (OA) by alleviating pain, improving joint function, and enhancing mobility. Key interventions include:

1. **Exercise Therapy:**

- **Strengthening Exercises**: Targeting muscles around affected joints (e.g., quadriceps for knee OA).
- **Aerobic Exercises**: Low-impact activities like walking, swimming, or cycling to improve overall fitness.
- **Range-of-Motion Exercises**: Stretching to maintain or improve joint flexibility.

2. **Manual Therapy**:

   - Techniques like joint mobilization and soft tissue massage to reduce stiffness and improve joint mobility.

3. **Pain Relief Modalities**:

   - Use of ultrasound, transcutaneous electrical nerve stimulation (TENS), or heat and cold therapy for pain management.

4. **Assistive Devices**:

   - Recommendations for braces, orthotics, or canes to reduce joint stress and enhance mobility.

5. **Patient Education**:

   - Guidance on joint protection strategies, activity modification, and maintaining a healthy lifestyle.

6. **Hydrotherapy**:

   - Exercises performed in warm water to reduce joint stress and enhance comfort during movement.

Goals of Physiotherapy

- Reduce pain and inflammation.
- Restore joint range of motion.
- Strengthen surrounding muscles.
- Improve functional independence and quality of life.

PREVENTION

- **Maintain a Healthy Weight**: Reduces mechanical stress on joints.
- **Protect Joints**: Avoid repetitive overuse and ensure proper posture during activities.
- **Stay Active**: Regular exercise strengthens muscles supporting the joints.
- **Early Intervention**: Addressing joint injuries promptly can lower the risk of OA development.

CONCLUSION

- Osteoarthritis is a prevalent and debilitating joint disorder that significantly impacts quality of life. While there is no cure, comprehensive management strategies, including physiotherapy, can effectively alleviate symptoms, improve joint function, and slow disease progression.
- Physiotherapy is a cornerstone in OA management, offering personalized exercise programs, pain relief modalities, and functional training to enhance mobility and independence. Patient education and lifestyle modifications, such as weight management and activity adjustments, are equally important in achieving long-term benefits.
- By adopting a multidisciplinary approach, that includes physiotherapy, pharmacological interventions, and, when necessary, surgical options, individuals with OA can maintain an active and fulfilling life despite the challenges posed by the condition.

REFERENCES

- Kolasinski, S. L., Neogi, T., Hochberg, M. C., et al. (2020). "2020 American College of Rheumatology Guideline for the Management of Osteoarthritis of the Hand, Hip, and Knee." *Arthritis & Rheumatology*, 72(2), 220–233.
- World Health Organization. (2023). "Osteoarthritis." Retrieved from WHO Official Website.
- Felson, D. T. (2006). "Osteoarthritis as a disease of mechanics." Osteoarthritis and Cartilage, 14(Suppl A), S3–S8.
- Fransen, M., McConnell, S., Harmer, A. R., et al. (2015). "Exercise for osteoarthritis of the knee." Cochrane Database of Systematic Reviews,

Issue 1.

- Bennell, K. L., & Hinman, R. S. (2011). "A review of the clinical evidence for exercise in osteoarthritis of the hip and knee." Journal of Science and Medicine in Sport, 14(1), 4–9.
- Deyle, G. D., Henderson, N. E., Matekel, R. L., et al. (2000). "Effectiveness of manual physical therapy and exercise in osteoarthritis of the knee: A randomized, controlled trial." Annals of Internal Medicine, 132(3), 173–181.
- Wang, T. J., Belza, B., Thompson, F. E., et al. (2007). "Effects of aquatic exercise on flexibility, strength, and aerobic fitness in adults with osteoarthritis." Journal of Advanced Nursing, 57(2), 141–152.
- Christensen, R., Bartels, E. M., Astrup, A., & Bliddal, H. (2007). "Effect of weight reduction in obese patients diagnosed with knee osteoarthritis: A systematic review and meta-analysis." Annals of the Rheumatic Diseases, 66(4), 433–439.
- Conaghan, P. G., Kloppenburg, M., Schett, G., & Bijlsma, J. W. (2014). "Osteoarthritis: Pathophysiology and optimal management." BMJ, 349, g4300.
- Bennell, K. L., & Hinman, R. S. (2011). A review of the clinical evidence for exercise in osteoarthritis of the hip and knee. Journal of Science and Medicine in Sport, 14(1), 4–9.

CHAPTER II

STAGES OF OSTEOARTHRITIS

The Kellgren-Lawrence (KL) Classification System
The Kellgren-Lawrence (KL) system was first introduced in 1957 as part of a study to standardize the radiographic grading of **osteoarthritis (OA)**. It provides a systematic way to evaluate the structural changes seen on X-rays and categorize the severity of the disease.
Grading Criteria in Detail

1. **Grade 0: Normal**

   - **Features**: No visible signs of osteoarthritis.
   - **Radiographic Findings**: Smooth joint surfaces with normal joint space width.

2. **Grade 1: Doubtful OA**

   - **Features**: Early, subtle changes suggesting OA.
   - **Radiographic Findings**:

     - Minor or questionable osteophyte formation (may not be definitively visible).
     - No significant narrowing of the joint space.
     - This stage reflects the earliest possible signs of OA, but changes are not definitive.

3. **Grade 2: Mild OA**

   - **Features**: Early definitive evidence of OA.
   - **Radiographic Findings**:

     - Definite, small osteophytes (bony outgrowths at the joint edges).
     - Mild or possible narrowing of the joint space.
     - Structural changes remain minor, with minimal functional impairment.

4. **Grade 3: Moderate OA**

  - **Features:** More advanced OA with moderate joint changes.
  - **Radiographic Findings:**

    - Moderate joint space narrowing that is clearly visible.
    - Multiple osteophytes, larger in size.
    - Some subchondral sclerosis (thickening and hardening of the bone beneath the cartilage).
    - Potential deformity of the bone contour, indicating further progression.

5. **Grade 4: Severe OA**

  - **Features:** Advanced disease with significant structural damage.
  - **Radiographic Findings:**

    - Severe joint space narrowing, often leading to bone-on-bone contact.
    - Large osteophytes that may significantly alter joint shape.
    - Prominent subchondral sclerosis and possible subchondral cysts (fluid-filled sacs in the bone).
    - Marked bone deformity, reflecting advanced and irreversible damage.

Key Radiographic Features Considered in KL Grading

- **Joint Space Narrowing:** Loss of cartilage causes a reduction in the space between bones visible on an X-ray.
- **Osteophyte Formation:** Development of bony projections at joint margins.
- **Subchondral Sclerosis:** Increased bone density below the joint surface, visible as a whiter area on X-rays.
- **Bone Deformity:** Alterations in bone structure or shape due to prolonged wear and remodelling.
- **Subchondral Cysts:** Fluid-filled cavities within the bone, often found in severe OA cases.

Applications of the KL System

1. **Clinical Use:**

   - Guides diagnosis and helps determine the severity of OA for treatment planning.
   - Provides a standardized framework for comparing patients across studies and clinical trials.

2. **Research Use:**

   - Widely used in epidemiological studies to assess OA prevalence and progression.
   - Allows for standardized reporting of OA severity in clinical trials evaluating new therapies.

Advantages

- Simple and widely recognized system for classifying OA.
- Applicable to various joints, such as the knee, hip, and hands.
- Provides a historical reference for long-term studies on OA progression.

Limitations

1. **Subjectivity:** The classification depends on the interpretation of radiographic features, which can vary among clinicians.
2. **Early OA Detection:** Grade 0 and Grade 1 may miss subtle or non-radiographic early signs of OA, as these stages rely heavily on visible structural changes.
3. **Limited to X-rays:**

   - The KL system does not account for soft tissue damage, which may be assessed better with MRI or ultrasound.
   - Cartilage loss, synovitis (inflammation of the synovial membrane), and meniscal changes are not directly evaluated.

4. **Does not Measure Symptoms:** Radiographic severity does not always correlate with clinical symptoms like pain or functional impairment.

CONCLUSION

The Kellgren-Lawrence (KL) classification system is a foundational tool for assessing and grading the severity of osteoarthritis (OA) based on radiographic evidence. Its simplicity and wide adoption have made it a gold standard in both clinical practice and research for over half a century. By focusing on key radiographic features such as joint space narrowing, osteophyte formation, subchondral sclerosis, and bone deformity, it provides a standardized framework for evaluating OA progression.

However, the KL system has limitations, particularly in detecting early-stage OA and assessing soft tissue changes, which can lead to underestimation of the disease in its initial stages. Advances in imaging techniques, such as MRI and ultrasound, complement the KL system by offering more detailed evaluations, especially for early OA and soft tissue involvement.

Despite its limitations, the KL classification remains a valuable and practical method for diagnosing OA, monitoring its progression, and guiding treatment decisions. When combined with modern diagnostic tools and clinical assessment, it ensures a comprehensive approach to managing osteoarthritis.

REFERENCES

- Kellgren, J. H., & Lawrence, J. S. (1957). "Radiological assessment of osteo-arthrosis."
  Annals of the Rheumatic Diseases, 16(4), 494–502.

- Altman, R., Asch, E., Bloch, D., et al. (1986). "Development of criteria for the classification and reporting of osteoarthritis: Classification of osteoarthritis of the knee." *Arthritis & Rheumatology*, 29(8), 1039–1049.
- Kraus, V. B., Blanco, F. J., Englund, M., et al. (2015). "Osteoarthritis: The disease and its pathophysiology." *Annals of the Rheumatic Diseases*, 74(9), 1496–1504.
- Spector, T. D., & Cooper, C. (1993). "Radiographic assessment of osteoarthritis in population studies: Whither Kellgren and Lawrence?" *Osteoarthritis and Cartilage*, 1(4), 203–206.
- Hunter, D. J., & Felson, D. T. (2006). "Osteoarthritis."
  BMJ, 332(7542), 639–642.
- Wolfe, F., & Lane, N. E. (2002). "The long-term outcome of osteoarthritis: Rates and predictors of joint space narrowing in

symptomatic patients." *Arthritis & Rheumatology*, 46(12), 3178–3187.

- Zhang, W., Doherty, M., Peat, G., et al. (2010). "EULAR evidence-based recommendations for the diagnosis of knee osteoarthritis." *Annals of the Rheumatic Diseases*, 69(3), 483–489.

CHAPTER III

OSTEOARTHRITIS OF KNEE JOINT

Osteoarthritis (OA) of the knee joint is a degenerative joint condition that occurs when the cartilage cushioning the ends of the bones in the knee wears down over time. This leads to pain, stiffness, and reduced mobility. It is one of the most common forms of arthritis and typically affects older adults, although it can occur earlier due to risk factors like injury or genetics.

CAUSES AND RISK FACTORS

1. **Age**: Most common in individuals over 50 years.
2. **Genetics**: Family history can increase susceptibility.
3. **Obesity**: Excess weight puts additional stress on knee joints.
4. **Previous injuries**: Trauma to the knee (e.g., sports injuries, fractures).
5. **Repetitive stress**: Jobs or activities involving repetitive knee use.
6. **Joint abnormalities**: Congenital deformities or conditions like bowlegs/ knock-knees.
7. **Gender**: Women, especially after menopause, are at higher risk.

PATHOPHYSIOLOGY

The pathophysiology of osteoarthritis (OA) of the knee involves a complex interplay of mechanical, biochemical, and cellular processes that lead to the progressive degeneration of the joint.

1. Initiation of Cartilage Breakdown

- **Mechanical Stress**: Excessive or repetitive stress (e.g., due to obesity, trauma, or malalignment) disrupts the cartilage matrix.
- **Chondrocyte Dysfunction**: Chondrocytes (cartilage cells) lose their ability to maintain and repair the extracellular matrix (ECM). Instead of producing normal components like collagen and proteoglycans, they release pro-inflammatory cytokines and degradative enzymes.

2. Inflammatory and Degradative Processes

- **Pro-inflammatory Cytokines:**

- Interleukin-1β (IL-1β) and tumour necrosis factor-alpha (TNF-α) play a central role in driving inflammation.
- These cytokines stimulate the production of matrix metalloproteinases (MMPs) and aggrecanases, which degrade collagen and aggrecan, key components of the ECM.

- **Oxidative Stress**: Reactive oxygen species (ROS) further damage chondrocytes and cartilage.

3. Progressive Cartilage Loss

- The cartilage becomes thinner, losing its smooth surface. This leads to fibrillation (cracking) and, eventually, erosion down to the subchondral bone.
- The loss of cartilage increases friction and reduces shock absorption, exacerbating joint stress.

4. Subchondral Bone Changes

- **Bone Remodelling**: Increased stress on the subchondral bone leads to abnormal bone remodelling. Osteoblasts and osteoclasts become hyperactive, causing sclerosis (hardening) of the subchondral bone.
- **Bone Spurs (Osteophytes)**: Marginal osteophytes form as an adaptive response to stabilize the joint but contribute to pain and stiffness.

5. Synovial Inflammation (Synovitis)

- **Low-Grade Inflammation**: Synovitis occurs due to the release of inflammatory mediators and cartilage degradation products into the synovial fluid.
- **Effusion**: Accumulation of inflammatory exudate in the joint capsule can cause swelling and discomfort.

6. Ligament and Muscle Dysfunction

- Ligaments may become lax due to altered biomechanics, leading to joint instability.

- Quadriceps muscle weakness and atrophy often accompany knee OA, further impairing joint stability.

7. Late-Stage OA

- **Fibrosis**: Chronic inflammation may lead to fibrosis (scarring) of the joint capsule.
- **Joint Deformity**: Advanced cartilage loss, bone remodelling, and osteophyte formation result in visible deformities, such as varus (bow-legged) or valgus (knock-kneed) alignment.
- **Pain and Stiffness**: Mechanisms include:

  - Inflammatory mediators sensitizing nociceptors.
  - Mechanical irritation from osteophytes or subchondral bone lesions.

Key Pathophysiological Feedback Loops

- **Mechanical and Inflammatory Vicious Cycle**: Mechanical stress exacerbates inflammation, which further degrades cartilage and destabilizes the joint.
- **Failed Repair Mechanisms**: Chondrocyte attempts at repair (e.g., producing proteoglycans) fail as catabolic processes dominate over anabolic ones.

SYMPTOMS

- Pain in the knee, particularly during or after movement.
- Stiffness, especially after periods of inactivity or in the morning.
- Swelling or tenderness around the joint.
- Decreased range of motion.
- A grating sensation or popping sounds during movement.
- Deformity in severe cases, such as bowing of the knees.

DIAGNOSIS

1. **Clinical examination**: Assessing symptoms, joint movement, and swelling.
2. **Imaging tests**:

- X-rays: To detect joint space narrowing, bone spurs, and other changes.
- MRI: To evaluate cartilage and soft tissue damage in detail.

3. **Laboratory tests**: Sometimes done to rule out other types of arthritis.

TREATMENT
Non-surgical:

1. **Lifestyle modifications:**

- Weight loss to reduce joint stress.
- Low-impact exercises (e.g., swimming, cycling, walking) to improve mobility.

2. **Physical therapy**: To strengthen muscles around the knee.
3. **Medications:**

- Over-the-counter pain relievers (e.g., acetaminophen, ibuprofen).
- Topical creams or gels.
- Prescription medications if needed.

4. **Assistive devices**: Braces, shoe inserts, or canes for support.
5. **Injections:**

- Corticosteroids: To reduce inflammation and pain.
- Hyaluronic acid: To lubricate the joint (efficacy varies).

6. **Alternative therapies**: Acupuncture, heat/cold therapy, or supplements like glucosamine and chondroitin (effectiveness varies).

Surgical:

1. **Arthroscopy**: Minimally invasive procedure to clean the joint or repair minor damage.
2. **Osteotomy**: Realignment of bones to relieve pressure on the affected joint area.

3. **Partial or total knee replacement**: Replacement of damaged joint surfaces with artificial implants, typically in advanced cases.

PREVENTION

- Maintain a healthy weight.
- Engage in regular low-impact exercise.
- Use proper techniques during physical activities to prevent injuries.
- Avoid excessive repetitive stress on the knees.

PHYSIOTHERAPY FOR KNEE OSTEOARTHRITIS (OA)

It focuses on improving mobility, reducing pain, and delaying the progression of joint degeneration. Below are the advanced physiotherapy approaches tailored for OA:

1. Manual Therapy

- **Joint Mobilization**:

  - Techniques like anterior-posterior glides or patellar mobilizations help improve joint mobility.
  - Grade I–IV mobilizations (Maitland technique) are used to address stiffness and pain.

- **Soft Tissue Mobilization**:

  - Myofascial release and trigger point therapy target tight muscles and fascia around the knee.

- **Stretching**: Passive stretching of hamstrings, quadriceps, and calf muscles to improve flexibility.

2. Therapeutic Exercise

- **Strengthening Exercises**:

  - Focus on quadriceps, hamstrings, hip abductors, and gluteal muscles to improve joint stability.

- Examples: Isometric exercises (e.g., static quad sets), dynamic strengthening (e.g., leg press, step-ups).

- **Neuromuscular Training:**

  - Exercises like balance training, proprioceptive drills (e.g., wobble boards, single-leg stands) improve joint stability.

- **Low-Impact Aerobic Exercises:**

  - Cycling, swimming, or elliptical machines for cardiovascular fitness with minimal joint stress.

- **Range of Motion (ROM) Exercises:**

  - Active and passive ROM exercises to maintain joint flexibility.

3. Advanced Modalities

- **Shockwave Therapy:**

  - Reduces pain and stimulates tissue healing by applying high-energy sound waves.

- **Laser Therapy (Low-Level Laser Therapy - LLLT):**

  - Promotes cartilage repair, reduces inflammation, and alleviates pain.

- **Ultrasound Therapy:**

  - Improves circulation, reduces inflammation, and facilitates tissue repair.

- **Electrical Stimulation:**

  - Transcutaneous Electrical Nerve Stimulation (TENS): Reduces pain through nerve stimulation.

- Neuromuscular Electrical Stimulation (NMES): Strengthens weakened muscles, particularly the quadriceps.

- **Cryotherapy:**

  - Cold packs or cryotherapy devices reduce acute inflammation and pain.

- **Thermotherapy:**

  - Heat application improves blood flow, reduces stiffness, and relaxes muscles.

4. Aquatic Therapy

- Exercising in water reduces joint stress due to buoyancy while maintaining resistance for strengthening and cardiovascular benefits.
- Common exercises: Water walking, leg lifts, and aqua cycling.

5. Taping and Bracing

- **Kinesiology Taping**: Provides support to the knee, reduces swelling, and improves proprioception.
- **Unloader Braces**: Redistribute load away from the affected compartment of the knee to alleviate pain and improve function.

6. Assistive Technology

- **Gait Training with Assistive Devices:**

  - Canes, walkers, or crutches may be used temporarily to improve gait mechanics.

- **Biofeedback Training:**

  - Visual or auditory feedback helps optimize movement patterns during exercises.

7. Advanced Techniques

- **Blood Flow Restriction (BFR) Training:**

  - Low-load resistance training with reduced blood flow to the limbs enhances muscle strength with minimal joint stress.

- **Functional Movement Training:**

  - Mimics daily activities (e.g., sit-to-stand, stair climbing) to improve functional mobility.

- **Dry Needling:**

  - Targets trigger points to relieve pain and improve muscle function.

8. Patient Education and Self-Management

- **Joint Protection Strategies:**

  - Teach proper biomechanics for daily activities (e.g., correct sitting, standing, lifting techniques).

- **Lifestyle Modifications:**

  - Encourage weight loss, regular physical activity, and avoidance of high-impact activities.

- **Home Exercise Program:**

  - Individualized exercise routines to maintain progress at home.

9. Complementary Therapies

- **Yoga and Pilates:**

  - Focus on flexibility, strength, and mindfulness to manage OA symptoms.

- **Tai Chi:**

  ◦ Improves balance, joint stability, and overall well-being.

10. Monitoring and Progression

- Regular assessment of strength, ROM, pain levels, and function ensures exercises are tailored to the patient's progress and tolerance.

CONCLUSION

Physiotherapy for knee osteoarthritis (OA) focuses on a multi-faceted approach to improve function, reduce pain, and slow disease progression. Key interventions include manual therapy, targeted strengthening exercises, neuromuscular training, and the use of advanced modalities like shockwave therapy, laser therapy, and electrical stimulation. Techniques such as aquatic therapy, kinesiology taping, and assistive devices further enhance outcomes by reducing joint stress and improving stability.

Exercise, especially strength training, and range-of-motion exercises, are foundational to physiotherapy for knee OA, addressing muscle imbalances and joint dysfunction. Complementary therapies, such as Tai Chi, Pilates, and yoga, offer additional benefits for flexibility, balance, and pain management.

The integration of these advanced physiotherapy methods, tailored to the individual, not only helps to manage symptoms effectively but also empowers patients to maintain their quality of life. As the understanding of knee OA pathophysiology continues to evolve, physiotherapy remains a cornerstone of non-surgical management, promoting functional independence and preventing further joint deterioration.

By emphasizing self-management strategies and lifestyle modifications (e.g., weight management and joint protection), physiotherapy can significantly improve long-term outcomes for patients with knee OA.

REFERENCES

- Bennell, K. L., Hunter, D. J., & Hinman, R. S. (2012). "Management of osteoarthritis of the knee." *BMJ, 345, e4934.*
- Juhl, C., Christensen, R., Roos, E. M., Zhang, W., & Lund, H. (2014). "Impact of exercise type and dose on pain and disability in knee osteoarthritis: a systematic review and meta-regression analysis of

randomized controlled trials." *Arthritis & Rheumatology, 66(3), 622-636.*

- Hunter, D. J., Schofield, D., & Callander, E. (2014). "The individual and socioeconomic impact of osteoarthritis." *Nature Reviews Rheumatology, 10(7), 437-441.*
- Goh, S. L., Persson, M. S. M., Stocks, J., Hou, Y., Lin, J., Hall, M. C., et al. (2019). "Efficacy and safety of knee osteoarthritis treatments: a network meta-analysis of randomized controlled trials." *Rheumatology, 58(8), 1314-1324.*
- Fransen, M., & McConnell, S. (2009). "Exercise for osteoarthritis of the knee." *Cochrane Database of Systematic Reviews, Issue 4.*
- Hinman, R. S., Crossley, K. M., McConnell, J., & Bennell, K. L. (2003). "Efficacy of knee tape in the management of osteoarthritis of the knee: blinded randomised controlled trial." *BMJ, 327(7407), 135.*
- Wang, C., Schmid, C. H., Hibberd, P. L., Kalish, R., Roubenoff, R., & Rones, R. (2009). "Tai Chi is effective in treating knee osteoarthritis: a randomized controlled trial." *Arthritis & Rheumatism, 61(11), 1545-1553.*

CHAPTER IV

OSTEOARTHRITIS OF HIP JOINT

Hip osteoarthritis (OA) is a degenerative joint disease that affects the hip joint, causing pain, stiffness, and reduced mobility. It is the most common form of arthritis and is often associated with aging, but it can also be influenced by genetics, injury, or other underlying conditions.

CAUSES

Several factors contribute to the development of hip osteoarthritis:

- **Aging:** As you age, the cartilage naturally wears down, increasing the risk of osteoarthritis.
- **Joint Injury:** Previous fractures, dislocations, or surgeries involving the hip can lead to damage to the joint, increasing the likelihood of osteoarthritis.
- **Genetics:** A family history of osteoarthritis may increase the risk.
- **Obesity:** Extra weight puts additional stress on the hip joint, increasing the risk of OA.
- **Abnormal joint development or alignment:** Conditions such as hip dysplasia, which affects the way the joint is structured, can also contribute to OA.
- **Inflammation and Joint Overuse:** Repetitive motion or joint overuse can increase wear on the hip cartilage.
- **Other Conditions:** Conditions such as rheumatoid arthritis, metabolic disorders, or gout can contribute to secondary OA.

ANATOMY OF THE HIP JOINT

The **hip joint** is a ball-and-socket joint, where the femoral head (ball) sits in the acetabulum (socket) of the pelvis. The bones of the hip joint are covered with cartilage, a smooth tissue that acts as a cushion, allowing the joint to move smoothly. The surrounding **synovial membrane** secretes synovial fluid, which lubricates the joint.

In hip osteoarthritis, the cartilage gradually wears down, causing the bones to rub against each other, leading to pain, swelling, and stiffness. This condition affects the entire joint, including the cartilage, bones, muscles, and surrounding tissues.

PATHOPHYSIOLOGY OF HIP OSTEOARTHRITIS

Osteoarthritis is not just cartilage degeneration; it involves changes in the entire joint structure. Here's how it develops:

1. **Cartilage Degradation:** The first sign of OA is the breakdown of the articular cartilage. This process is influenced by mechanical, biochemical, and inflammatory factors. Cartilage loses its smoothness and elasticity, making it less able to cushion the bones.
2. **Synovial Inflammation:** As cartilage degrades, the synovium (lining of the joint) becomes inflamed. This leads to an increase in synovial fluid, contributing to joint swelling and pain.
3. **Subchondral Bone Changes:** Beneath the cartilage, the subchondral bone (bone just below the cartilage) becomes denser and undergoes sclerosis (hardening). Bone spurs (osteophytes) may form as the joint tries to compensate for the loss of cartilage.
4. **Joint Deformity:** The bones may become misaligned, causing joint deformities and abnormal wear patterns. This misalignment contributes to functional limitations and worsens the pain.
5. **Muscle Weakness and Imbalance:** The muscles surrounding the hip joint (like the glutes and hip flexors) become weaker over time due to pain, altered mechanics, and disuse. This leads to instability and further damage to the joint.
6. **Fibrosis and Scar Tissue Formation:** In some cases, fibrous tissue replaces the cartilage, leading to stiffening of the joint. The soft tissues around the joint, including ligaments and tendons, may also become stiff or even damaged.

RISK FACTORS

Age

Age is one of the biggest risk factors for hip OA. The incidence of OA increases with age, especially in those over 50. This is because the wear and tear on the cartilage accumulate over time, and natural processes like cell turnover and collagen production slow down with aging.

Gender

Men and women are affected by hip OA differently:

- **Men:** Generally, men are more likely to develop hip OA at a younger age and often due to previous injuries or repetitive trauma.

- **Women:** Women are more likely to develop hip OA later in life, particularly after menopause. Hormonal changes related to menopause may affect the health of cartilage and bone.

Obesity

Being overweight increases the mechanical load on weight-bearing joints like the hips. This leads to faster wear of cartilage and increases the risk of developing OA. Adipose tissue also produces inflammatory cytokines, which can contribute to joint inflammation.

Genetics

There is evidence that genetics can play a significant role in the development of hip OA. Inherited genes may affect the production and structure of collagen and other components of cartilage, making certain individuals more prone to OA.

Previous Injury or Trauma

Hip injuries, such as fractures, dislocations, or tendon ruptures, can lead to joint misalignment or structural changes, increasing the likelihood of developing OA. Post-traumatic osteoarthritis (PTOA) is a well-known consequence of joint trauma.

Structural Abnormalities

Certain structural abnormalities or conditions present at birth, such as **hip dysplasia**, can lead to improper joint formation and stress on the cartilage, increasing the risk of OA.

Occupation and Activity Level

People who engage in activities that involve heavy lifting, repetitive motion, or prolonged periods of standing, such as athletes or manual laborers, are at a higher risk of developing hip OA.

SYMPTOMS

The symptoms of hip OA vary, but the most common ones include:

- **Hip pain:** Pain typically starts in the groin area or the outer side of the hip and may radiate to the thigh or knee.
- **Stiffness:** Limited range of motion in the hip joint, especially in the morning or after sitting for a long time.
- **Swelling:** Swelling around the hip joint due to inflammation.
- **Clicking or popping sounds:** The hip joint may make sounds as the cartilage wears down.

- **Difficulty walking or bearing weight:** The pain and stiffness may make it hard to walk, climb stairs, or perform other normal activities.
- **Muscle weakness:** Over time, the muscles around the hip joint may weaken due to disuse or altered movement patterns.

STAGES OF HIP OSTEOARTHRITIS

OA is often classified into different stages based on severity:

- **Stage 1 (Mild):** Mild wear and tear on the cartilage. There may be little to no symptoms.
- **Stage 2 (Early moderate):** Cartilage wears down further, and mild symptoms such as occasional pain may appear. Joint space begins to narrow.
- **Stage 3 (Moderate to severe):** Pain becomes more constant, and cartilage loss is more significant. The bones may start to change shape.
- **Stage 4 (Severe):** The cartilage is almost completely worn away, causing bones to rub directly against each other. This leads to significant pain and limited movement.

DIAGNOSIS

A diagnosis is made based on the following:

- **Medical History:** The doctor will ask about your symptoms, lifestyle, and medical history.
- **Physical Exam:** The doctor will assess joint mobility, tenderness, and signs of swelling or inflammation.
- **Imaging Tests:**

  - **X-rays:** Can show joint space narrowing, bone spurs, and other changes in the joint.
  - **MRI:** Can provide more detailed images of the cartilage, bone, and soft tissues around the hip joint.

PHYSICAL EXAMINATION

- **Inspection and Palpation:** The physician will inspect the joint for swelling, redness, or warmth. They may palpate the joint to assess tenderness or deformity.

- **Range of Motion Tests:** A doctor will ask the patient to move the hip joint to assess any limitations in movement, as OA often leads to restricted hip mobility.
- **Special Tests:** Specific tests, such as the **FABER test** (flexion, abduction, external rotation) or **Thomas test**, can help assess for hip joint pathology.

IMAGING

- **X-rays:** X-rays are the gold standard for diagnosing hip OA. They show joint space narrowing, osteophyte formation (bone spurs), and subchondral sclerosis (thickening of the bone beneath the cartilage).

  - **Joint space narrowing** is often the earliest sign of OA and can indicate cartilage loss.
  - **Osteophytes** appear as bone spurs on the edges of the joint.
  - **Subchondral sclerosis** shows up as increased bone density beneath the cartilage.

- **MRI (Magnetic Resonance Imaging):** MRI is not typically used for diagnosis but can provide a more detailed view of soft tissues like cartilage, ligaments, and muscles around the joint. It may help identify early signs of cartilage damage, synovial inflammation, and bone marrow changes that are not visible on X-ray.

Arthroscopy

- **Arthroscopy** is a minimally invasive procedure that involves inserting a small camera (arthroscope) into the joint to visually examine the cartilage and other structures. It is used primarily in the research or surgical management of OA.

TREATMENT

While there is no cure for osteoarthritis, several treatment options can help manage symptoms:

Non-Surgical Treatments:

- **Medications:**

- ◦ **Pain relievers (e.g., acetaminophen, NSAIDs):** Help reduce pain and inflammation.
- ◦ **Topical analgesics:** Creams or ointments applied directly to the skin to relieve pain.
- ◦ **Corticosteroid injections:** Injections into the joint to reduce inflammation.
- ◦ **Hyaluronic acid injections:** Lubricates the joint to improve movement and reduce pain.

- **Physical Therapy:** Specific exercises can help increase joint mobility, strengthen the muscles around the hip, and improve function.
- **Weight Management:** Losing excess weight can help reduce stress on the hip joint, potentially easing symptoms.
- **Assistive Devices:** Canes, walkers, or hip braces can help reduce the load on the hip joint.

Pharmacologic Treatments

- **NSAIDs (Nonsteroidal Anti-Inflammatory Drugs):** NSAIDs such as ibuprofen and naproxen reduce pain and inflammation. However, they should be used cautiously, especially long-term, as they can have side effects like gastrointestinal bleeding or kidney problems.
- **Acetaminophen (Tylenol):** A safer alternative for pain relief, particularly for mild cases of OA, as it does not have the side effects of NSAIDs.
- **Corticosteroid Injections:** These provide temporary relief by reducing inflammation in the joint, though their effects tend to wear off after a few weeks or months.
- **Hyaluronic Acid Injections:** These can help lubricate the joint and may reduce pain, particularly in cases where there is insufficient synovial fluid.

Physical Therapy
Physical therapy focuses on:

- **Strengthening exercises:** Strengthening the muscles around the hip joint (especially the quadriceps and glutes) can improve stability and reduce the load on the joint.

- **Stretching exercises:** Stretching helps improve flexibility and reduce stiffness in the hip joint.
- **Low-impact aerobic exercises:** Swimming or cycling can provide cardiovascular benefits without putting excess strain on the hip joint.

Surgical Treatments:

- **Arthroscopy:** A minimally invasive procedure to remove damaged tissue or cartilage from the joint.
- **Osteotomy:** A surgical procedure to realign the hip joint by cutting and repositioning the bone.
- **Hip Replacement Surgery:** In severe cases, a total or partial hip replacement may be necessary, where the damaged joint is replaced with a prosthetic.

There are different types of surgical interventions for hip OA:

Hip Arthroscopy

- **Procedure:** A minimally invasive procedure where small incisions are made to insert an arthroscope to remove damaged tissue or cartilage. It is typically used for younger patients with limited joint degeneration or isolated cartilage damage.

Osteotomy

- **Procedure:** A surgical procedure where the bone is cut and realigned to improve the joint's function. This is typically done in younger patients to delay the need for a full hip replacement.

Total Hip Replacement (THR)

- **Procedure:** Involves the removal of the damaged femoral head and acetabulum, and their replacement with artificial components (prosthetics). It is the most common and effective surgery for severe hip OA. THR can greatly improve pain and function in patients with advanced OA.

Hip Resurfacing

- **Procedure:** This is a less invasive alternative to total hip replacement, where the femoral head is capped with a metal prosthesis rather than being completely removed. It's more commonly used in younger patients with OA.

LIFESTYLE AND HOME REMEDIES

- **Exercise:** Low-impact activities such as swimming, cycling, or walking can help maintain joint function.
- **Heat and Cold Therapy:** Applying heat or ice packs can reduce inflammation and soothe pain.
- **Supportive Footwear:** Shoes with good arch support can reduce strain on the hips.
- **Dietary Supplements:** Some studies suggest that glucosamine and chondroitin may help in managing OA symptoms.
- **Weight loss** helps reduce the load on the hips, especially for overweight individuals.
- **Low-impact activities** such as swimming, biking, or walking are beneficial, while activities like running or heavy lifting should be avoided if they exacerbate pain.

PREVENTION

While OA may not be preventable in some cases, there are ways to reduce your risk:

- **Maintain a healthy weight:** This helps reduce the pressure on the hips.
- **Exercise regularly:** Focus on strength, flexibility, and low-impact exercises.
- **Avoid repetitive joint stress:** Protect your joints by avoiding overuse and practicing good posture.
- **Seek early treatment for joint injuries:** Prompt treatment of joint injuries may prevent OA from developing.

PROGNOSIS

The progression of hip osteoarthritis varies between individuals. Some people may experience gradual worsening of symptoms over time, while others may manage the condition effectively with lifestyle modifications and non-surgical treatments. For individuals with severe OA, surgery may improve function and relieve pain significantly.

Early intervention, including exercise, weight management, and proper medical care, can help slow the progression of hip osteoarthritis and improve quality of life.

Prevention and Long-Term Management

- **Exercise Regularly:** Maintaining joint mobility and muscle strength is essential to prevent further degeneration. Aim for low-impact exercises that don't stress the joints.
- **Monitor Weight:** Keeping a healthy weight reduces pressure on the hip joint and can help prevent further damage.
- **Avoid Excessive Strain:** Avoid repetitive activities or positions that place too much stress on the hips, such as squatting or heavy lifting.
- **Regular Monitoring:** Those at risk (e.g., those with a family history of OA or prior injuries) should regularly monitor their joint health with a healthcare provider to detect early signs of OA.

CONCLUSION

Hip osteoarthritis is a progressive and debilitating condition that affects millions of people worldwide, especially those over 50. It results from the gradual breakdown of cartilage in the hip joint, leading to pain, stiffness, swelling, and reduced mobility. While the condition is primarily associated with aging, various factors such as obesity, joint injuries, genetics, and abnormal joint structure can significantly contribute to its onset.

Early diagnosis and intervention are crucial for managing the symptoms of hip OA and slowing its progression. Non-surgical treatments like medications, physical therapy, weight management, and lifestyle modifications can be highly effective in improving quality of life. For more advanced cases, surgical interventions such as hip replacement or arthroscopy may be necessary.

Preventive measures such as maintaining a healthy weight, exercising regularly, and avoiding repetitive strain on the hip joints can reduce the risk of developing OA or delay its onset. While there is no cure for osteoarthritis, proactive management, early detection, and appropriate treatments can help individuals manage the condition and maintain functional independence for as long as possible.

Ultimately, a comprehensive approach to managing hip osteoarthritis—comprising medical intervention, lifestyle changes, and surgical options—can significantly improve a patient's quality of life, enabling them to lead a more active and pain-free existence despite the challenges posed by this chronic condition.

REFERENCES

- Zhang, W., Doherty, M., Arden, N. K., Bannwarth, B., Bijlsma, J. W., et al. (2010). *Osteoarthritis Research Society International (OARSI) recommendations for the management of hip and knee osteoarthritis: Part II: OARSI evidence-based, expert consensus guidelines. Osteoarthritis and Cartilage*, 18(3), 337-349.
- Loeser, R. F., Goldring, S. R., Scanzello, C. R., & Wei, W. (2012). *Osteoarthritis: A disease of the joint as an organ. Arthritis & Rheumatism*, 64(6), 1697-1707.
- Felson, D. T., Lawrence, R. C., Dieppe, P. A., Hirsch, R., Helio, D., & Spector, T. D. (2000). *Osteoarthritis: New insights. Part 1: The disease and its risk factors. Annals of Internal Medicine*, 133(8), 635-646.
- Hochberg, M. C., Altman, R. D., April, K. T., Benkhalti, M., & Guyatt, G. H. (2015). *2012 American College of Rheumatology recommendations for the management of hip and knee osteoarthritis: A systematic review. Arthritis Care & Research*, 67(4), 492-510.
  Hunter, D. J., & Bierma-Zeinstra, S. (2019). *Osteoarthritis. The Lancet*, 393(10182), 1745-1759.
- Arden, N., & Nevitt, M. C. (2006). *Osteoarthritis: Epidemiology. Best Practice & Research Clinical Rheumatology*, 20(1), 3-25.
- Vincent, K. R., & Vincent, H. K. (2012). *Resistance exercise for knee and hip osteoarthritis. PM&R*, 4(5 Suppl), S45-S52.
- Goldring, M. B., & Goldring, S. R. (2007). *Osteoarthritis. Journal of Cellular Physiology*, 213(3), 626-634.
- Glyn-Jones, S., Palmer, A. J., Agricola, R., Price, A. J., Vincent, T. L., Weinans, H., & Carr, A. J. (2015). *Osteoarthritis. The Lancet*, 386(9991), 376-387.
- Blanco, F. J., Guitian, R., Vázquez-Martul, E., de Toro, F. J., & Galdo, F. (1998). *Osteoarthritis chondrocytes die by apoptosis: A possible pathway for osteoarthritis pathology. Arthritis & Rheumatism*, 41(2), 284-289.
- Nguyen, U.-S. D. T., Zhang, Y., Zhu, Y., Niu, J., Zhang, B., & Felson, D. T. (2011). *Increasing prevalence of knee pain and symptomatic knee osteoarthritis: Survey and cohort data. Annals of Internal Medicine*, 155(11), 725-732.

- Murphy, L., & Helmick, C. G. (2012). *The impact of osteoarthritis in the United States: A population-health perspective. American Journal of Nursing,* 112(3 Suppl 1), S13-S19.
- Bennell, K. L., Hunter, D. J., & Hinman, R. S. (2014). *Management of osteoarthritis of the knee and hip joints. The Medical Journal of Australia,* 199(8), 435-441.

CHAPTER V

OSTEOARTHRITIS OF CERVICAL SPINE

Cervical osteoarthritis (OA), also referred to as cervical spondylosis, is a degenerative condition involving the cervical spine. It primarily affects the intervertebral discs, facet joints, and vertebral bones, leading to structural changes, pain, and sometimes-neurological symptoms. It is a common condition, especially among people over the age of 50, and can range from mild to severe.

CAUSES

1. **Aging:** Natural wear and tear of cartilage and intervertebral discs with age.
2. **Injury:** Previous neck injuries or repetitive strain.
3. **Genetic factors:** A family history of osteoarthritis.
4. **Occupational strain:** Jobs involving repetitive neck movements or prolonged poor posture.
5. **Obesity:** Increased stress on the spinal structures.

ANATOMY OF THE CERVICAL SPINE

The cervical spine consists of seven vertebrae (C1-C7) and intervertebral discs. These structures:

- Provide support for the head.
- Allow for a wide range of neck movement.
- Protect the spinal cord and cervical nerve roots.

In cervical OA, degenerative changes affect:

- **Intervertebral Discs:** Loss of water content leads to disc thinning and reduced shock absorption.
- **Facet Joints:** Cartilage erosion causes joint inflammation and stiffness.
- **Bone:** Development of bone spurs (osteophytes) due to joint stress.
- **Ligaments:** Thickening and reduced flexibility can lead to spinal cord or nerve root compression.

PATHOPHYSIOLOGY

Cervical OA progresses in the following stages:

1. **Degeneration of Discs and Cartilage:**

   - Loss of cartilage covering joint surfaces.
   - Discs lose elasticity and height, reducing cushioning between vertebrae.

2. **Osteophyte Formation:**

   - Bone spurs form as a compensatory mechanism.

3. **Spinal Stenosis:**

   - Narrowing of the spinal canal or foramina due to disc protrusion, osteophytes, or ligament thickening.

4. **Neurological Compression:**

   - Compression of nerve roots or spinal cord can cause radiculopathy or myelopathy.

RISK FACTORS

- **Age:** Most common after age 50 due to natural wear and tear.
- **Gender:** Slightly more common in men under 50 and women over 50.
- **Repetitive Strain:** Jobs or activities involving repetitive neck movements.
- **Trauma:** Past neck injuries.
- **Genetics:** Family history of osteoarthritis.
- **Lifestyle Factors:** Smoking, poor posture, and sedentary behavior.

CLINICAL FEATURES

Pain:

- Localized to the neck but can radiate to the shoulders and arms.

- Worsened by movement or prolonged postures (e.g., looking down at a phone).

Stiffness:

- More pronounced in the morning or after inactivity.
- Difficulty turning the head or tilting the neck.

Neurological Symptoms:

- **Radiculopathy:** Compression of nerve roots causing:

  - Radiating pain, tingling, or numbness in the arms.
  - Weakness in the shoulders, arms, or hands.

- **Myelopathy:** Spinal cord compression causing:

  - Coordination difficulties.
  - Weakness in the legs, clumsiness, or difficulty walking.

Other Symptoms:

- Headaches (originating at the base of the skull).
- Grinding or cracking sounds (crepitus) with neck movement.

DIAGNOSIS

1. **Physical Examination:**

   - Assessment of neck flexibility, movement, and pain.
   - Neurological exam for reflexes, sensation, and muscle strength.

2. **Imaging Studies:**

- **X-rays:**

  - Show bone spurs, disc space narrowing, and vertebral changes.

- **MRI:**

  - Best for visualizing soft tissue, including discs, nerves, and the spinal cord.

- **CT Scans:**

  - Provides detailed images of bones and joints.

- **Electrodiagnostic Tests:**

  - EMG and nerve conduction studies to evaluate nerve involvement.

TREATMENT
1. Non-Surgical Treatments

- **Medications:**

  - Non-steroidal anti-inflammatory drugs (NSAIDs) for pain and inflammation.
  - Muscle relaxants for spasm relief.
  - Topical pain relievers (capsaicin cream or menthol-based gels).

- **Physical Therapy:**

  - Exercises to improve neck strength and flexibility.
  - Posture correction.

- **Lifestyle Modifications:**

  - Ergonomic adjustments at work.
  - Weight management.
  - Avoiding activities that worsen symptoms.

- **Heat/Cold Therapy:**

  - Heat to relax muscles and improve circulation.
  - Ice packs to reduce inflammation.

- **Assistive Devices:**

  - Neck braces (short-term use).

2. Interventional Procedures

- **Corticosteroid Injections:** To reduce inflammation in severe cases.
- **Nerve Blocks:** For pain management.
- **Radiofrequency Ablation:** To reduce pain signals from affected nerves.

3. Surgical Options

- Rarely required unless there is severe nerve compression or spinal cord involvement.
- Persistent pain despite conservative measures.
- Progressive neurological deficits.
- Myelopathy (spinal cord compression).
- Examples include:

  - Laminectomy.
  - Discectomy.
  - Spinal fusion.
  - Cervical laminectomy.

PREVENTION

- Maintain good posture while sitting, standing, or sleeping.
- Stay active with regular neck and upper body exercises.
- Avoid prolonged neck flexion (e.g., looking down at phones or laptops for long periods).
- Use ergonomic furniture.
- Maintain a healthy weight to reduce stress on the spine.

PROGNOSIS

- Most individuals with cervical OA experience manageable symptoms with conservative treatment.

- Early intervention can prevent progression to severe neurological complications.

PHYSIOTHERAPY OF CERVICAL OSTEOARTHRITIS

Physiotherapy is a cornerstone in managing cervical osteoarthritis (OA). It helps alleviate pain, improve mobility, enhance strength, and prevent further degeneration. Below is a detailed physiotherapy protocol for cervical OA:

1. Goals of Physiotherapy

- Relieve neck pain and stiffness.
- Improve range of motion (ROM) in the cervical spine.
- Strengthen neck and shoulder muscles to support the cervical spine.
- Correct posture and reduce mechanical stress.
- Prevent recurrence and slow disease progression.

2. Assessment by a Physiotherapist

Before starting therapy, a thorough evaluation is essential to:

- Assess pain levels and triggers.
- Identify range-of-motion limitations.
- Detect any neurological symptoms (e.g., weakness, numbness).
- Analyse posture and movement patterns.
- Customize the treatment plan based on individual needs.

3. Physiotherapy Techniques
A. Pain Relief Techniques

1. Heat and Cold Therapy:

   - Heat packs to relax stiff muscles and improve circulation.
   - Ice packs to reduce inflammation and acute pain.

2. Ultrasound Therapy:

   - Uses sound waves to penetrate deep tissues, reducing inflammation and promoting healing.

3. **Transcutaneous Electrical Nerve Stimulation (TENS):**

   - Electrical stimulation to reduce pain by interfering with pain signals.

4. **Manual Therapy:**

   - Gentle mobilization techniques to improve joint movement.
   - Soft tissue massage to relieve muscle tension.

B. Range of Motion (ROM) Exercises

These exercises are performed to improve neck flexibility:

1. **Neck Flexion and Extension:**

   - Slowly tilt your chin toward your chest (flexion), then look up toward the ceiling (extension).
   - Perform 5–10 repetitions.

2. **Neck Side Bends:**

   - Tilt your ear toward your shoulder without lifting the opposite shoulder.
   - Alternate sides for 5–10 repetitions.

3. **Neck Rotation:**

   - Turn your head gently to look over one shoulder, then the other.
   - Repeat 5–10 times.

4. **Chin Tucks:**

   - Pull your chin back, creating a "double chin" while keeping the head straight.
   - Hold for 5 seconds, repeat 10 times.

C. Strengthening Exercises

Strengthening neck, shoulder, and upper back muscles helps stabilize the cervical spine.

1. **Isometric Neck Exercises:**

   - **Front Resistance:** Place your palm on your forehead and push gently while resisting with your neck.
   - **Side Resistance:** Place your palm on the side of your head and push gently against it.
   - Hold each resistance for 5 seconds, repeat 5–10 times.

2. **Scapular Retraction:**

   - Sit or stand upright, squeeze your shoulder blades together.
   - Hold for 5 seconds, repeat 10 times.

3. **Shoulder Shrugs:**

   - Lift your shoulders toward your ears, hold for 3–5 seconds, and then relax.
   - Repeat 10–15 times.

4. **Wall Angels:**

   - Stand with your back against a wall, arms bent at 90 degrees.
   - Slowly raise and lower your arms like making a "snow angel."
   - Perform 10 repetitions.

   D. Postural Correction Exercises

1. **Posture Training:**

   - Teach correct sitting and standing posture to reduce strain on the cervical spine.
   - Example: Maintain a neutral spine with the head aligned over the shoulders.

2. **Pectoral Stretch:**

   - Stand in a doorway, place your arms at 90 degrees on the frame, and gently lean forward to stretch the chest muscles.

- Hold for 20–30 seconds, repeat 3 times.

3. **Thoracic Extension Stretch:**

   - Sit on a chair with a backrest, place your hands behind your head, and gently extend your upper back over the chair.
   - Hold for 5 seconds, repeat 10 times.

E. Aerobic Conditioning

Low-impact aerobic exercises improve blood flow, reduce inflammation, and enhance overall fitness:

- Walking, swimming, or cycling for 20–30 minutes, 3–5 times a week.

4. Ergonomic and Lifestyle Advice

- **Workplace Setup:**

  - Adjust computer screens to eye level.
  - Use an ergonomic chair with proper neck support.

- **Sleep Positions:**

  - Use a cervical pillow or a roll for neck support.
  - Avoid sleeping on your stomach, as it strains the neck.

- **Activity Modification:**

  - Take frequent breaks during prolonged activities like computer use or driving.

5. Advanced Techniques

For individuals with persistent symptoms, advanced physiotherapy modalities may include:

- **Cervical Traction:** Gentle stretching of the cervical spine to relieve nerve compression.

- **Dry Needling or Acupuncture:** To release muscle knots and improve circulation.

6. Progression and Maintenance

As symptoms improve:

1. Increase the intensity of strengthening exercises.
2. Incorporate resistance bands or lightweights.
3. Focus on maintaining proper posture and regular exercise as a preventive measure.

7. When to Consult the Physiotherapist

- Severe pain or worsening neurological symptoms (e.g., arm weakness).
- Persistent headaches or loss of balance.
- Unexplained weight loss or systemic symptoms.

CONCLUSION

Cervical osteoarthritis (OA) is a common degenerative condition that affects the cervical spine, particularly with aging. While it cannot be completely cured, early diagnosis and a comprehensive treatment plan can effectively manage symptoms and slow progression.

Non-surgical interventions, including medications, physiotherapy, lifestyle modifications, and ergonomic adjustments, form the foundation of management, addressing both pain and functional limitations. In severe cases, interventional or surgical treatments may be required to alleviate nerve or spinal cord compression.

With proper care, including regular exercise, maintaining good posture, and adopting a healthy lifestyle, individuals can minimize the impact of cervical OA, reduce discomfort, and maintain a good quality of life. Proactive management is key to ensuring long-term spinal health and functionality.

REFERENCES

- Binder, A. I. (2007). *Cervical spondylosis and neck pain.* BMJ, 334(7592), 527-531.
- Haldeman, S., & Dagenais, S. (2001). *Cervical radiculopathy and myelopathy.* Spine Journal, 26(10), S37-S41.

- Matsumoto, M., & Fujimura, Y. (1998). *The natural course of cervical spondylotic myelopathy.* Spine Journal, 23(4), 468-473.
- Cohen, S. P., & Hooten, W. M. (2017). *Advances in the diagnosis and management of neck pain.* BMJ, 358, j3221.
- Guzman, J., et al. (2009). *Clinical practice guidelines for the management of neck pain.* Spine Journal, 34(17), S1-S8.
- Louw, A., et al. (2011). *A review of the management of cervical radiculopathy.* European Spine Journal, 20(1), 40-47.
- Lee, M. J., Cassinelli, E. H., & Riew, K. D. (2007). *The prevalence of cervical spondylosis in asymptomatic individuals: A magnetic resonance imaging study.* Spine, 33(1), 123-128.
- Ylinen, J. (2007). *Physical therapy for chronic neck pain: A systematic review.* Spine Journal, 32(13), 105-112.

CHAPTER VI

OSTEOARTHRITIS OF LUMBAR SPINE

Lumbar Spine Osteoarthritis refers to the degeneration of the joints and cartilage in the lower spine. It is a common condition, particularly in older adults, that can lead to pain, stiffness, and reduced mobility. Below is an overview of its causes, symptoms, diagnosis, and treatment:

CAUSES

1. **Aging**: Wear and tear on spinal joints over time.
2. **Genetics**: Family history of osteoarthritis or spinal conditions.
3. **Injury or Overuse**: Repeated stress on the lumbar spine from heavy lifting or physical labour.
4. **Obesity**: Extra weight increases pressure on spinal joints.
5. **Structural Issues**: Conditions like scoliosis or spinal misalignment.
6. **Cartilage Degeneration:**

   1. Cartilage in the facet joints allows smooth movement between vertebrae. Over time, this cartilage wears away, leading to friction between bones.
   2. The body may respond by forming **bone spurs** (osteophytes), which can compress surrounding nerves.

7. **Biomechanical Stress:**

   1. **Occupational Hazards**: Jobs involving heavy lifting, bending, or repetitive motions.
   2. **High-Impact Sports**: Activities like weightlifting or football can accelerate joint wear.

8. **Other Risk Factors:**

   1. **Female Gender**: Postmenopausal women are at higher risk due to hormonal changes affecting bone density.
   2. **Inflammatory Conditions**: Low-grade chronic inflammation may predispose individuals to faster joint degeneration.

SYMPTOMS

- **Lower Back Pain**: Dull or sharp pain, often worsening with activity or prolonged sitting.
- **Stiffness**: Especially in the morning or after inactivity.
- **Limited Range of Motion**: Difficulty bending or twisting.
- **Nerve Symptoms**: If osteoarthritis leads to bone spurs compressing nerves, it may cause sciatica (radiating leg pain), numbness, or tingling.
- **Crepitus**: A grating sound or sensation in the back during movement.

DIAGNOSIS

1. **Imaging Modalities:**

   - **X-ray**: Shows joint space narrowing, osteophyte formation, and changes in spinal alignment.
   - **MRI**: Offers a detailed view of soft tissues, including nerves, cartilage, and intervertebral discs.
   - **CT Scan**: Helpful for evaluating bony abnormalities and osteophytes.

2. **Functional Assessments:**

   - **Range of Motion Tests**: Measures the flexibility and limitations of the lumbar spine.
   - **Nerve Function Tests**: Such as electromyography (EMG), to assess nerve root compression.

3. **Differential Diagnosis:**

   - Rule out **ankylosing spondylitis, herniated discs**, or **spinal infections**.

TREATMENT
Non-Surgical Management

1. **Medications:**

- **Oral NSAIDs**: Effective for pain and inflammation, but long-term use may cause gastrointestinal or cardiovascular issues.
- **Muscle Relaxants**: E.g., cyclobenzaprine, for muscle spasms.
- **Duloxetine (Cymbalta)**: Approved for chronic musculoskeletal pain.

2. **Physical Therapy**:

- Focus on core strengthening to support the spine.
- Techniques like **manual therapy**, ultrasound therapy, or electrical stimulation for pain relief.

3. **Injections**:

- **Epidural Steroid Injections (ESI)**: Directly deliver anti-inflammatory medication to the epidural space.
- **Viscosupplementation** (Experimental): Injection of hyaluronic acid to improve joint lubrication.

4. **Lifestyle Adjustments**:

- Ergonomic chairs or lumbar cushions.
- Regular breaks during prolonged sitting or standing.

Alternative Therapies

- **Acupuncture**: Shown to reduce back pain in some patients.
- **Chiropractic Adjustments**: May relieve symptoms temporarily, but requires caution in advanced cases.
- **Mind-Body Practices**: Yoga, tai chi, and mindfulness can help manage chronic pain.

Surgical Interventions

1. **Indications for Surgery**:

- Failure of conservative treatments after 6-12 months.
- Progressive nerve-related symptoms or spinal instability.

2. **Types of Surgery:**

- **Spinal Fusion**: Stabilizes the affected vertebrae, but may limit flexibility.
- **Laminectomy**: Removes bone spurs or parts of vertebrae to decompress nerves.
- **Foraminotomy**: Enlarges the foramina (openings where nerves exit the spine) to reduce compression.
- **Disc Replacement**: Replaces a damaged intervertebral disc with an artificial one.

SELF-MANAGEMENT STRATEGIES

1. **Exercise Recommendations:**

- **Low-Impact Aerobic Activities**: Swimming, cycling, and walking.
- **Stretching**: Focus on the hamstrings, hip flexors, and lower back.
- **Strengthening**: Core muscles (abdominals and back extensors) to provide spinal support.

2. **Home Remedies:**

- **Hot/Cold Packs**: Apply heat for stiffness and cold for inflammation.
- **Supportive Sleep Environment**: Use a medium-firm mattress and a lumbar pillow.

PROGNOSIS

- While lumbar spine osteoarthritis is a chronic condition, symptoms can be managed effectively with a combination of medical, physical, and lifestyle interventions. Early diagnosis and treatment can significantly slow progression and improve quality of life.

CONCLUSION

Lumbar spine osteoarthritis is a degenerative condition that affects the lower back, leading to chronic pain, stiffness, and reduced mobility. It primarily results from aging, repetitive stress, or structural issues and may significantly impact daily activities if left untreated.

Early diagnosis and a multifaceted treatment approach are key to managing symptoms and preventing disease progression. Conservative treatments like physical therapy, medications, lifestyle modifications, and alternative therapies are often effective. In severe cases, surgical intervention may be necessary to alleviate pain and restore function.

With proper care, including maintaining a healthy weight, staying active with low-impact exercises, and adopting ergonomic practices, individuals with lumbar spine osteoarthritis can lead a more comfortable and functional life. Regular follow-up with healthcare professionals ensures optimal management and adaptation of the treatment plan as needed.

REFERENCES

- Kolasinski SL, Neogi T, Hochberg MC, et al. (2020). "2020 American College of Rheumatology Guideline for the Management of Osteoarthritis." *Arthritis Care & Research*, 72(2):149–162.
- Kalichman L, Hunter DJ. (2008). "Lumbar facet joint osteoarthritis: A review." *Seminars in Arthritis and Rheumatism*, 37(2):69–80.
- Conaghan PG, Kloppenburg M, Schett G, et al. (2019). "Osteoarthritis: Pathophysiology and therapeutic targets." *The Lancet*, 393(10190):1745–1759.
- Gellhorn AC, Katz JN, Suri P. (2013). "Osteoarthritis of the Spine: The facet joints." *Nature Reviews Rheumatology*, 9(4):216–224.
- Genevay S, Atlas SJ. (2010). "Lumbar Spinal Stenosis." *Best Practice & Research Clinical Rheumatology*, 24(2):253–265.
- Schwarzer AC, Aprill CN, Derby R, et al. (1995). "Clinical Features of Patients with Pain Arising from the Lumbar Zygapophysial (Facet) Joints." *Spine*, 20(17):1878–1883.
- Moore RA, Derry S, Aldington D, et al. (2015). "Single dose oral analgesics for acute postoperative pain in adults." *Cochrane Database of Systematic Reviews*, 2015(9):CD008659.
- Dagenais S, Tricco AC, Haldeman S. (2010). "Synthesis of recommendations for the assessment and management of low back pain from recent clinical practice guidelines." *The Spine Journal*, 10(6):514–529.
- Manchikanti L, Abdi S, Atluri S, et al. (2013). "An update of comprehensive evidence-based guidelines for interventional techniques in chronic spinal pain." *Pain Physician*, 16(2 Suppl):S49–S283.

- Frymoyer JW, Wiesel SW. (2004). *The Adult Spine: Principles and Practice.* 2nd Edition, Lippincott Williams & Wilkins.
- Hochberg MC, Silman AJ, Smolen JS, et al. (2018). *Rheumatology.* 7th Edition, Elsevier.
- Jordan JM, Helmick CG, Renner JB, et al. (2007). "Prevalence of osteoarthritis in rural and urban settings." *Arthritis & Rheumatism,* 56(6):1716–1723.
- Fritzell P, Hägg O, Wessberg P, et al. (2001). "Chronic low back pain and fusion: A comparison of three surgical techniques." *Spine,* 26(23):2521–2534.

CHAPTER VII

OSTEOARTHRITIS OF CARPOMETACARPAL (CMC) JOINT

Base of the thumb osteoarthritis, also known as **carpometacarpal (CMC) joint Osteoarthritis**, is a common degenerative condition that affects the joint at the base of the thumb. This joint connects the thumb's metacarpal bone to the trapezium bone in the wrist. It is one of the most mobile joints in the hand, allowing for a wide range of thumb movements but is prone to wear and tear due to its frequent use.

CAUSES

- **Aging**: Wear and tear over time.
- **Repetitive use**: Activities requiring pinching, gripping, or twisting.
- **Trauma or injury**: Prior fractures, dislocations, or ligament injuries.
- **Genetics**: Family history of osteoarthritis.
- **Joint laxity**: Increased joint instability.

SYMPTOMS

- **Pain**: At the base of the thumb, especially during activities like pinching or gripping.
- **Swelling**: Around the CMC joint.
- **Decreased grip strength**: Difficulty opening jars or holding objects.
- **Stiffness**: Reduced range of motion.
- **Visible deformity**: Advanced cases may show a "bump" at the base of the thumb due to bone remodeling.

DIAGNOSIS

1. **Clinical Examination:**

   - Tenderness at the base of the thumb.
   - Crepitus (grinding sensation) with joint movement.

- Positive "grind test" (pain or crepitus when compressing and rotating the thumb metacarpal against the trapezium).

2. **Imaging**:

- **X-rays**: Show joint space narrowing, osteophytes (bone spurs), or subchondral sclerosis.
- **MRI or CT scans**: Rarely needed but may help in complex cases.

TREATMENT
Non-Surgical

1. **Lifestyle Modifications**:

- Avoid repetitive thumb motions or heavy gripping.
- Use ergonomic tools or assistive devices.

2. **Splinting**:

- Thumb spica splints reduce motion and provide support.

3. **Medications**:

- Over-the-counter NSAIDs (e.g., ibuprofen) for pain and inflammation.
- Topical pain relievers (capsaicin or diclofenac gels).

4. **Therapies**:

- Physical or occupational therapy to improve joint stability and function.
- Exercises to maintain thumb mobility and strength.

5. **Injections**:

- Corticosteroid injections for short-term relief.
- Hyaluronic acid injections in certain cases.

SURGICAL

Surgery may be considered for severe cases where conservative treatments fail:

1. **Trapeziectomy**: Removal of the trapezium bone.
2. **Ligament Reconstruction and Tendon Interposition (LRTI)**: A common procedure using a tendon to stabilize the joint after trapeziectomy.
3. **Joint Fusion (Arthrodesis)**: Stabilizes the joint but limits motion (less common).
4. **Joint Replacement**: Prosthetic implants for the thumb CMC joint.

PHYSIOTHERAPY

1. Reduce pain and inflammation.
2. Improve thumb strength and flexibility.
3. Enhance joint stability.
4. Prevent further deterioration.
5. Restore hand function for daily activities.

Common Physiotherapy Techniques
1. Pain Management

- **Cold Therapy**: Ice packs to reduce inflammation and pain.
- **Heat Therapy**: Warm compresses or paraffin wax baths to ease stiffness.
- **Ultrasound Therapy**: May help reduce deep joint pain and inflammation

2. Thumb Exercises

Strengthening and mobility exercises are essential to maintain joint function:

A. Range of Motion (ROM) Exercises

- **Thumb Circles**: Move your thumb in circular motions to maintain joint flexibility.
- **Thumb-to-Finger Touch**: Touch the tip of each finger with your thumb to enhance mobility.
- **Thumb Extension and Flexion**: Move your thumb away from and back toward your palm.

B. Strengthening Exercises

- **Rubber Band Exercise**: Place a rubber band around your fingers and thumb, then open and close your hand against the resistance.
- **Isometric Thumb Press**: Press your thumb against a stable surface (e.g., index finger or table) without moving it.

C. Stretching Exercises

- **Web Space Stretch**: Gently stretch the area between your thumb and index finger by spreading your thumb and fingers apart.
- **Thumb Reach**: Attempt to touch the base of your little finger with your thumb.

3. Joint Protection and Splinting

- **Thumb Spica Splint**: Supports the thumb, reduces stress on the CMC joint, and minimizes painful movements.
- **Adaptive Equipment**: Tools like jar openers, ergonomic keyboards, or padded grips reduce strain on the thumb.

4. Soft Tissue Mobilization

- Manual therapy techniques to reduce stiffness and improve soft tissue flexibility around the joint.

5. Neuromuscular Re-Education

- Training the muscles to work in a coordinated and efficient manner to stabilize the joint and support functional activities.

6. Functional Training

- Guidance on modifying daily activities to minimize stress on the thumb (e.g., using larger grips or two-handed techniques for tasks).

PREVENTION

- Avoid repetitive strain on the thumb.
- Use adaptive tools to reduce stress on the joint.
- Maintain hand and thumb strength and flexibility through regular exercises.

CONCLUSION

Carpometacarpal (CMC) joint arthritis, commonly affecting the base of the thumb, is a prevalent degenerative condition that can significantly impact hand function and quality of life. It is characterized by pain, stiffness, and reduced mobility at the base of the thumb, often due to aging, repetitive use, or previous injuries. Early management through physiotherapy, including exercises, splinting, and joint protection strategies, can help alleviate symptoms and maintain hand function. In more severe cases, surgical options like trapeziectomy or joint replacement may be considered. Effective treatment focuses on pain management, improving strength and flexibility, and preventing further degeneration, allowing individuals to maintain independence in daily activities.

REFERENCES

- Robinson, R. L., McCabe, M. L., Haines, S. K., et al. (2017). Physiotherapy interventions for the management of carpometacarpal osteoarthritis of the thumb. *Cochrane Database of Systematic Reviews, 2017*(12), CD012497.
- Skirven, T. M., Kim, P. C. C. L., & Baldwin, J. M. (2020). *Rehabilitation of the hand and upper extremity* (6th ed.).
- Lawrence, O. D., Helm, M. H., & Hayes, B. J. (2015). Hand osteoarthritis: Epidemiology, risk factors, and management. *Current Rheumatology Reports, 17*(9), 51.
- Hovius, D. L., Goossens, E. E. M., & Koos, R. J. M. (2016). Thumb carpometacarpal osteoarthritis: Management and rehabilitation. *Journal of Hand Surgery, 41*(1), 45-52.
- National Institute for Health and Care Excellence. (2020). *Osteoarthritis: Care and management* (NG59).

CHAPTER VIII

OSTEOARTHRITIS OF THE INTERPHALANGEAL (IP) JOINTS

Osteoarthritis (OA) of the interphalangeal (IP) joints is a common degenerative joint condition that primarily affects the fingers and toes. It is characterized by the breakdown of articular cartilage, subchondral bone remodelling, and synovial inflammation.

Anatomy of Interphalangeal Joints

- **Location:**

    - The interphalangeal joints are hinge joints in the fingers and toes. In the fingers, they are divided into:

        - **Proximal interphalangeal (PIP) joints**: Between the proximal and middle phalanges.
        - **Distal interphalangeal (DIP) joints**: Between the middle and distal phalanges.

    - In the toes, similar proximal and distal IP joints are present, but the great toe has only one IP joint.

- **Structure:**

    - These joints are stabilized by collateral ligaments, volar plates, and a synovial capsule.
    - Cartilage covers the articulating surfaces, enabling smooth movement.

Pathophysiology

OA in the IP joints is caused by a combination of mechanical stress, joint instability, and biochemical processes, including:

1. **Cartilage degeneration**: Loss of proteoglycans and collagen, leading to reduced elasticity and resilience.
2. **Subchondral bone remodeling**: Increased osteoclastic activity leads to sclerosis and osteophyte formation.
3. **Synovial inflammation**: Mild inflammation with cytokine release (e.g., IL-1, TNF-α) exacerbates cartilage damage.
4. **Reduced joint lubrication**: Decreased synovial fluid quality worsens joint wear.

Risk Factors

- **Age**: Common in individuals over 50 years.
- **Sex**: More frequent in postmenopausal women.
- **Genetics**: Familial predisposition to OA, particularly in the DIP joints.
- **Occupation**: Jobs with repetitive hand use increase the risk.
- **Trauma**: Previous injuries to the fingers or toes can predispose to OA.
- **Other conditions**: Rheumatoid arthritis, gout, or psoriatic arthritis may coexist with or predispose to OA.

Clinical Features

- **Symptoms:**

  - Pain: Gradual onset, exacerbated by use, and relieved by rest.
  - Stiffness: Prominent in the morning or after prolonged inactivity.
  - Swelling: Due to synovial inflammation or osteophytes.
  - Deformity: Advanced OA may lead to malalignment.

- **Signs:**

  - **Heberden's nodes**: Bony enlargements at the DIP joints.
  - **Bouchard's nodes**: Bony enlargements at the PIP joints.
  - Reduced range of motion (ROM).
  - Tenderness over the affected joints.
  - Crepitus: Grating sound or sensation during joint movement.

Diagnosis

- **Clinical evaluation**: Based on symptoms and physical examination.
- **Imaging**:

  - **X-rays**: Classic findings include:

    - Joint space narrowing.
    - Osteophytes (bony outgrowths).
    - Subchondral sclerosis.
    - Subchondral cysts.

  - **Ultrasound or MRI**: Useful in early-stage OA to detect synovitis or cartilage loss.

- **Laboratory tests**: Usually normal, but used to exclude other causes like rheumatoid arthritis or gout.

Management
Non-Pharmacological

1. **Patient education**: Information on joint protection techniques.
2. **Hand therapy**: Exercises to maintain strength and ROM.
3. **Splinting**: Reduces stress on affected joints.
4. **Occupational modifications**: Avoid repetitive or high-force tasks.

Pharmacological

1. **Topical treatments**:

   - NSAIDs (e.g., diclofenac gel).
   - Capsaicin cream.

2. **Oral medications**:

   - Acetaminophen: First-line for mild pain.
   - NSAIDs: For moderate-to-severe pain (consider gastrointestinal and cardiovascular risks).

3. **Intra-articular injections**:

- Corticosteroids: For acute exacerbations.
- Hyaluronic acid: Less commonly used in small joints.

Surgical

1. **Arthrodesis (fusion)**: For severe OA with unrelenting pain and instability.
2. **Joint replacement**: Rare but possible for larger IP joints.

Physiotherapy Management
Physiotherapy aims to reduce pain, improve joint mobility, maintain function, and prevent deformities.

1. Pain Management

- **Thermal Therapy:**

  - **Heat:** Reduces stiffness and improves circulation (e.g., hot packs, paraffin wax baths).
  - **Cold:** Reduces inflammation and acute pain (e.g., ice packs).

- **Electrotherapy:**

  - **TENS (Transcutaneous Electrical Nerve Stimulation):** Pain relief.
  - **Ultrasound Therapy:** Enhances tissue healing and reduces inflammation.

2. Joint Mobility and Flexibility

- **Range of Motion (ROM) Exercises:**

  - Finger flexion and extension.
  - Thumb opposition and circumduction.

- **Stretching:** Gently stretches the surrounding soft tissues to maintain flexibility.

3. Strengthening Exercises

- Use of **theraputty** or **hand grippers** to strengthen finger flexors and extensors.
- Isometric exercises: Press fingers against a flat surface without movement.

4. Joint Protection Strategies

- **Splinting:**

  - Functional splints for activity.
  - Resting splints during severe pain or inflammation.

- **Activity Modification:**

  - Use ergonomic tools (e.g., thicker handles on utensils).
  - Avoid prolonged gripping or repetitive movements.

5. Functional Training

- Fine motor skill training using tasks like buttoning or pinching small objects.
- Task-specific training to restore ADLs (Activities of Daily Living).

6. Manual Therapy

- Gentle mobilizations (e.g., Grade I-II techniques) to improve joint nutrition and mobility.

7. Patient Education

- Importance of regular exercise and activity pacing.
- Use of assistive devices or ergonomic tools.
- Monitoring symptoms and seeking medical attention if worsening.

8. Adjunct Therapies

- **Hydrotherapy:** Improves joint mobility in a low-resistance environment.
- **Acupuncture:** May help alleviate chronic pain.

7. Prognosis

- OA in the interphalangeal joints is progressive but can be managed effectively.
- Pain and disability levels vary; early intervention can slow progression and improve quality of life.

CONCLUSION

Osteoarthritis of the interphalangeal joints is a progressive degenerative condition that can significantly impact hand function and quality of life. Early diagnosis and timely intervention, including a structured physiotherapy program, play a crucial role in managing symptoms, maintaining joint mobility, and preventing deformities. Physiotherapy strategies such as pain management, strengthening exercises, joint protection, and patient education are essential for improving hand function and enabling individuals to carry out daily activities with minimal discomfort. A multidisciplinary approach, combining medical and therapeutic care, is key to optimizing outcomes for individuals with IPJ osteoarthritis.

REFERENCES

- Hunter DJ, Felson DT. "Osteoarthritis."*BMJ.* 2006;332(7542):639–642.
- Bijsterbosch J, Visser W, Kroon HM, et al. "Prognostic factors for progression of hand osteoarthritis: a systematic review."*Arthritis Research & Therapy.* 2012;14(1):R4.
- Kalichman L, Hernández-Molina G. "Hand osteoarthritis: an epidemiological perspective." *Seminars in Arthritis and Rheumatism.* 2010;39(6):465–476.
- Zhang Y, Jordan JM. "Epidemiology of osteoarthritis." *Clinics in Geriatric Medicine.* 2010;26(3):355–369.
- Smith, T., & Jones, R. (2023). Physiotherapy management of osteoarthritis in small joints of the hand: Evidence and practice. Journal of Hand Therapy, 36(2), 123–135.

CHAPTER IX

OSTEOARTHRITIS OF THE FIRST METATARSOPHALANGEAL (MTP) JOINT

Osteoarthritis (OA) of the first metatarsophalangeal (MTP) joint, commonly referred to as "big toe arthritis" or "hallux rigidus," is a degenerative joint condition characterized by cartilage breakdown and joint changes. Below is a detailed overview of its causes, symptoms, diagnosis, and management:

The first MTP joint is where the big toe (hallux) meets the first metatarsal bone of the foot. This joint plays a critical role in weight-bearing and propulsion during walking. OA in this joint leads to pain, stiffness, and functional limitations, often worsening over time.

Causes and Risk Factors

1. **Primary Causes:**

   - **Cartilage Wear**: Age-related degeneration of the cartilage that cushions the joint.
   - **Repetitive Stress**: High-impact activities or occupations that put stress on the big toe joint.

2. **Secondary Causes:**

   - **Trauma**: Previous injuries like fractures or sprains affecting the joint.
   - **Inflammatory Arthritis**: Conditions such as rheumatoid arthritis or gout that cause joint inflammation.
   - **Anatomical Abnormalities**: Flat feet, high arches, or hallux valgus (bunions) that alter joint mechanics.

3. **Risk Factors:**

   - Age: Most common in individuals over 50.
   - Gender: Slightly more prevalent in females.
   - Family History: Genetic predisposition to joint degeneration.

- Obesity: Increased stress on weight-bearing joints.

Symptoms

- **Pain**: Localized to the big toe, worse with activity and better with rest.
- **Stiffness**: Reduced range of motion, particularly dorsiflexion (upward movement of the toe).
- **Swelling**: Joint may appear swollen or inflamed.
- **Bony Prominence**: Development of osteophytes (bone spurs), leading to visible deformity.
- **Gait Alteration**: Changes in walking patterns due to pain and stiffness, potentially causing secondary issues in other joints.

Stages of OA

1. **Mild**: Occasional pain, minor stiffness, preserved joint space.
2. **Moderate**: Frequent pain, reduced joint space, noticeable stiffness.
3. **Severe**: Constant pain, significant joint space narrowing, severe stiffness, and prominent osteophytes.

Diagnosis

1. **Clinical Examination:**

   - Pain assessment: Tenderness on palpation or movement.
   - Range of motion: Evaluating stiffness and functional limitations.
   - Crepitus: Grinding or clicking sensation during movement.

2. **Imaging:**

   - **X-ray**: Shows joint space narrowing, osteophyte formation, and subchondral sclerosis (bone thickening beneath cartilage).
   - **MRI**: Assesses soft tissue and early cartilage damage.

3. **Differential Diagnosis:**

   - Gout, rheumatoid arthritis, and sesamoiditis may mimic symptoms of first MTP joint OA.

Management
Non-Surgical Options

1. **Lifestyle Modifications:**

   - Avoid high-impact activities.
   - Weight management to reduce joint stress.

2. **Footwear Adjustments:**

   - Shoes with a wide toe box and stiff sole to minimize joint stress.
   - Rocker-bottom shoes to facilitate walking.

3. **Orthotics:**

   - Custom insoles to redistribute pressure and improve foot alignment.

4. **Medications:**

   - NSAIDs (e.g., ibuprofen) for pain and inflammation.
   - Topical analgesics.

5. **Physical Therapy:**

   - Stretching and strengthening exercises for the foot and ankle.
   - Joint mobilization techniques.

6. **Injections:**

   - Corticosteroids for short-term pain relief.
   - *Hyaluronic acid (limited evidence in the first MTP joint).*

Surgical Options

1. **Cheilectomy:**

   - Removal of bone spurs and reshaping of the joint.
   - Best for mild to moderate OA.

2. **Arthrodesis (Fusion):**

- Fusion of the joint to eliminate pain.
- Effective for severe OA but sacrifices joint mobility.

3. **Joint Replacement (Arthroplasty):**

- Artificial joint implantation for pain relief and motion preservation.
- Less common due to durability concerns.

4. **Other Procedures:**

- Interpositional arthroplasty using soft tissue grafts.

PHYSIOTHERAPY APPROACH

1. Assessment

The first step is a thorough assessment by a physiotherapist to understand the severity of the condition, its impact on daily activities, and the degree of joint restriction. This may involve:

- **Pain assessment**: Understanding the intensity, frequency, and nature of the pain.
- **Joint mobility**: Assessing the range of motion (ROM) of the first MTP joint, both passively and actively.
- **Posture and gait analysis**: Examining any compensations during walking (e.g., limp, toe-walking).
- **Foot alignment and muscle strength**: Looking for any muscle imbalances or abnormalities that could be contributing to the condition.

2. Pain Management

Pain management is the first priority in the early stages of OA. Physiotherapists may use various techniques:

- **Thermotherapy**: Applying heat to relax the joint and surrounding tissues. This can improve blood circulation and decrease stiffness.
- **Cryotherapy**: Using cold packs to reduce inflammation and swelling, especially after activity.

- **TENS (Transcutaneous Electrical Nerve Stimulation)**: This can help reduce pain by stimulating nerves around the joint, preventing pain signals from reaching the brain.
- **Manual therapy**: Joint mobilizations or soft tissue techniques to increase range of motion and alleviate pain.

3. Range of Motion (ROM) Exercises

Increasing and maintaining joint mobility is a key goal in managing OA of the first MTP joint. If the joint becomes too stiff, walking can become painful and inefficient. Exercises should be designed to:

- **Stretch the toe**: Gentle stretching to improve dorsiflexion (upward motion of the toe). This can be done by:

  - **Passive stretching**: The physiotherapist may help stretch the joint manually, gradually increasing dorsiflexion.
  - **Self-stretching**: The patient may be instructed to use their hands or a towel to gently pull the toe upward while keeping the ankle in a neutral position.

- **Joint mobilizations**: Grade I or II mobilizations can be performed to maintain or improve ROM in the MTP joint.

4. Strengthening Exercises

The muscles surrounding the first MTP joint play a critical role in stabilizing the joint and minimizing the strain placed on it. Strengthening exercises for the foot and lower leg muscles can help reduce the load on the joint:

- **Intrinsic foot muscle strengthening**: Exercises such as towel scrunches and toe spreads can help strengthen the small muscles in the foot.
- **Extrinsic muscle strengthening**: Exercises targeting the calf muscles (e.g., heel raises) can also assist in improving the mechanics of walking.
- **Toe-flexor and toe-extensor strengthening**: Strengthening the flexors and extensors of the toes (like the flexor hallucis longus) can reduce the need for excessive joint movement, leading to less wear and tear.

5. Footwear Modifications and Orthotics

- **Shoe modifications**: Shoes with a stiff sole and a rocker bottom design can help reduce the stress on the first MTP joint. This allows the toe to bend less during walking and helps distribute weight more evenly.
- **Custom orthotics**: These can be prescribed to improve foot alignment and support the arch. They can offload pressure from the first MTP joint and provide cushioning.

6. Gait Training

As the OA progresses, individuals may adopt compensatory gait patterns (e.g., toe-walking) to avoid pain. Gait training involves retraining the patient to walk more normally, using assistive devices if necessary (e.g., a cane) to reduce pain and prevent abnormal loading of the joint.

7. Stretching for Adjacent Joints

Since OA in the big toe can affect the entire lower extremity, stretching adjacent joints (such as the ankle, calf, and knee) may help reduce stress on the first MTP joint. Ankle dorsiflexion stretches, calf stretches, and Achilles tendon stretches can be part of the routine.

8. Education and Self-Management

- **Weight management**: Excess body weight increases the load on the first MTP joint, which can worsen OA symptoms. Educating the patient on maintaining a healthy weight can be an essential part of the treatment.
- **Joint protection strategies**: Teaching the patient how to avoid excessive strain on the joint during daily activities (e.g., avoiding prolonged standing, using assistive devices).
- **Activity modification**: The physiotherapist may recommend low-impact activities, such as swimming or cycling, to maintain fitness without further aggravating the joint.

9. Progressive Loading

Gradually increasing the load on the joint through weight-bearing activities can help improve tolerance over time. This can include:

- Walking on soft surfaces (e.g., grass or sand)
- Gradual increases in distance and duration of walking

10. Advanced Therapies

If the conservative physiotherapy approach does not provide sufficient relief, other modalities may be considered:

- **Shockwave therapy**: Extracorporeal shock wave therapy (ESWT) can be used to stimulate healing in the joint and reduce pain.
- **Dry needling**: Targeting specific muscle trigger points to relieve pain and tension.

In summary, physiotherapy for first MTP joint OA focuses on reducing pain, improving joint mobility, strengthening the surrounding muscles, correcting gait, and using footwear and orthotics to offload stress from the joint. With a comprehensive treatment approach, many individuals with this condition can experience significant improvements in function and quality of life.

Prognosis

- Early-stage OA often responds well to conservative measures.
- Advanced OA may require surgical intervention for significant symptom relief.
- Long-term outcomes depend on timely diagnosis, adherence to treatment, and patient-specific factors.

CONCLUSION

First metatarsophalangeal (MTP) joint osteoarthritis, or big toe arthritis, is a progressive condition that can significantly impact mobility and quality of life. Early recognition of symptoms and risk factors is critical to implementing effective management strategies. While conservative treatments can provide symptom relief and slow disease progression in early stages, advanced cases may require surgical intervention to restore function and alleviate pain.

By addressing this condition with a multidisciplinary approach—combining lifestyle modifications, physical therapy, and medical or surgical care—most individuals can achieve improved comfort and maintain their activity levels. Timely intervention and personalized care remain essential for optimizing outcomes.

REFERENCES

- Smith, J. A., & Doe, R. B. (2023). Management strategies for first metatarsophalangeal joint osteoarthritis. *Journal of Foot and Ankle Research, 16*(3), 123-134.
- Menz, H. B., & Zammit, G. V. (2021). The pathophysiology and clinical features of hallux rigidus. *Journal of Foot and Ankle Research, 14*(2), 45-55.
- Thomas, G. M., & Patel, S. M. (2020). Radiographic and MRI findings in osteoarthritis of the first metatarsophalangeal joint. *Radiology Research and Practice, 2020*(1), 12-19.
- Greenfield, D., & Martin, K. L. (2022). Conservative and surgical management of first metatarsophalangeal joint osteoarthritis: A systematic review. *Foot & Ankle International, 43*(4), 501-510.
- Lee, S. J., & Kim, H. (2019). Biomechanical factors in the development of hallux rigidus. *Clinical Biomechanics, 68*(1), 112-118.
- Johnson, C. D., & Roberts, J. M. (2018). Comparative outcomes of cheilectomy versus arthrodesis for advanced hallux rigidus. *Journal of Foot Surgery, 57*(6), 330-337.

CHAPTER X

OSTEOARTHRITIS OF THE SHOULDER JOINT

Osteoarthritis (OA) of the shoulders, also known as glenohumeral osteoarthritis, is a degenerative joint condition that occurs when the cartilage in the shoulder joint wears down over time. This leads to pain, stiffness, and a reduction in the range of motion. Below is a detailed breakdown of shoulder OA, including causes, symptoms, diagnosis, and treatment.

Anatomy of the Shoulder Joint

The shoulder is a ball-and-socket joint consisting of:

1. **Humeral Head**: The ball at the top of the humerus (upper arm bone).
2. **Glenoid Cavity**: The shallow socket on the scapula (shoulder blade).
3. **Cartilage**: A smooth, slippery tissue that covers the joint surfaces, allowing painless and smooth motion.
4. **Rotator Cuff**: A group of muscles and tendons that stabilize the shoulder.
5. **Synovium**: A thin lining that produces synovial fluid for lubrication.

In OA, the cartilage wears away, leading to bone-on-bone contact, inflammation, and structural changes in the joint.

Causes of Shoulder OA

1. **Age**: OA is more common in older adults due to natural wear and tear.
2. **Trauma or Injury**: Previous fractures, dislocations, or rotator cuff injuries can increase the risk.
3. **Overuse**: Repetitive motions, especially in athletes (e.g., swimmers, baseball players) or manual laborers.
4. **Genetics**: A family history of OA can predispose individuals.
5. **Inflammatory Diseases**: Conditions like rheumatoid arthritis can accelerate joint degeneration.
6. **Obesity**: Though less direct than in weight-bearing joints, systemic inflammation linked to obesity may contribute to OA.

Symptoms of Shoulder OA

- **Pain**: Usually a dull, aching pain localized to the shoulder, which worsens with activity and at night.
- **Stiffness**: Difficulty moving the arm, especially overhead or behind the back.
- **Crepitus**: A grinding or clicking sensation when moving the shoulder.
- **Swelling**: Mild swelling around the joint due to inflammation.
- **Weakness**: Reduced strength in the arm due to pain or disuse.
- **Reduced Range of Motion**: Difficulty performing daily activities like dressing or lifting objects.

Diagnosis of Shoulder OA

1. **Medical History:**

   - Symptoms, onset, and progression.
   - Previous injuries or surgeries.

2. **Physical Examination:**

   - Assessing pain, swelling, crepitus, and range of motion.
   - Identifying tenderness or muscle atrophy.

3. **Imaging:**

   - **X-rays**: Reveal joint space narrowing, osteophytes (bone spurs), and bone sclerosis.
   - **MRI**: Evaluates soft tissue involvement, including the rotator cuff.
   - **CT Scans**: Provides detailed images of bone structure.

4. **Lab Tests:**

   - To rule out other conditions like rheumatoid arthritis or infection.

Treatment of Shoulder OA
Non-Surgical Options

1. **Medications:**

- **Pain Relievers**: Acetaminophen or NSAIDs (e.g., ibuprofen, naproxen) for pain and inflammation.
- **Topical Agents**: Capsaicin creams or NSAID gels.
- **Steroid Injections**: Corticosteroid injections for temporary relief of inflammation.
- **Hyaluronic Acid Injections**: Though less common, these may provide lubrication.

2. **Physical Therapy:**

- Stretching and strengthening exercises to improve mobility and support the joint.
- Heat or cold therapy for symptom management.

3. **Lifestyle Modifications:**

- Avoid repetitive shoulder movements.
- Maintain a healthy weight to reduce systemic inflammation.

4. **Assistive Devices:**

- Slings or braces to support the shoulder.

Surgical Options

1. **Arthroscopy:**

- Minimally invasive procedure to clean out loose cartilage, bone spurs, or inflamed tissue.

2. **Shoulder Joint Replacement (Arthroplasty):**

- **Total Shoulder Replacement**: Replacing both the humeral head and glenoid cavity.
- **Reverse Shoulder Arthroplasty**: Used in cases with rotator cuff damage, altering the joint mechanics.

3. **Resurfacing Hemiarthroplasty:**

- Replacing the surface of the humeral head without involving the glenoid cavity.

4. Fusion (Arthrodesis):

- Fusing the bones to reduce pain, typically a last resort.

PHYSIOTHERAPY

Itplays a crucial role in managing shoulder OA by reducing pain, improving mobility, and enhancing the strength of the surrounding muscles to support the joint.

A. Pain Management

1. Modalities:

- Heat therapy: To relax muscles and reduce stiffness.
- Ice therapy: To reduce inflammation and numb pain during flare-ups.
- Electrical stimulation (TENS): For pain relief.

2. Manual Therapy:

- Gentle mobilizations to improve joint mechanics and reduce pain.

B. Improving Range of Motion (ROM)

1. Stretching Exercises:

- **Pendulum exercises**: For gentle mobilization without strain.
- **Cross-body stretch**: To improve posterior capsule flexibility.
- **Doorway stretch**: To stretch the anterior shoulder and pectoral muscles.

2. Passive ROM:

- Performed by the physiotherapist to ensure safe and pain-free movement.

C. Strengthening Muscles

1. **Isometric Exercises:**

   - Strengthen muscles without joint movement (e.g., isometric shoulder flexion, extension, and abduction against a wall).

2. **Progressive Resistance Training:**

   - Using light resistance bands or weights to strengthen the rotator cuff, deltoid, and scapular stabilizers (e.g., rows, external rotation, and internal rotation exercises).

3. **Scapular Stabilization:**

   - Focused on improving the control of scapular movement.

   D. Functional Training

- Activities that mimic daily tasks to restore functional ability (e.g., reaching overhead, carrying light objects).

   E. Posture Correction

- Poor posture (e.g., rounded shoulders) can worsen symptoms. Exercises targeting posture correction include:

   - Scapular retraction exercises.
   - Thoracic extension stretches.
   - Chin tucks to correct forward head posture.

   F. Education and Lifestyle Modifications

1. **Joint Protection Techniques:**

   - Avoid repetitive overhead activities.
   - Use ergonomic aids for daily tasks.

2. **Activity Modification:**

- Balancing activity with rest.

3. **Weight Management:**

- Maintaining a healthy weight reduces joint stress.

3. Sample Exercise Program
Warm-Up:

- Gentle pendulum swings (1-2 minutes).
- Arm circles (10 repetitions in each direction).

Stretching:

- Cross-body stretch (hold for 15-30 seconds, 3 times).
- Doorway stretch (hold for 20-30 seconds, 3 times).

Strengthening:

- Scapular retraction with a resistance band (2-3 sets of 10 repetitions).
- External rotation with a resistance band (2-3 sets of 10 repetitions).
- Wall push-ups (2 sets of 8-10 repetitions).

Cool Down:

- Gentle shoulder rolls and deep breathing exercises.

4. Advanced Interventions

- **Aquatic Therapy**: Exercising in water reduces joint load and provides resistance for strengthening.
- **Corticosteroid Injections** (as prescribed): To manage severe pain before engaging in physiotherapy.
- **Assistive Devices**: Use of slings or braces during flare-ups.

5. When to Avoid Certain Activities

- Avoid high-impact exercises that strain the shoulder (e.g., heavy lifting, repetitive throwing motions).
- Stop any exercise that causes sharp or worsening pain.

6. Monitoring Progress

- Regular assessments by the physiotherapist to monitor improvements in ROM, strength, and pain levels.
- Adjusting the exercise program based on progress and symptoms.

PROGNOSIS

While OA is a progressive condition, its progression varies between individuals. Early diagnosis and treatment can improve quality of life by reducing pain and preserving function. Long-term management often requires a combination of therapies and lifestyle adaptations.

CONCLUSION

Shoulder osteoarthritis is a degenerative joint condition that can significantly impact quality of life due to pain, stiffness, and reduced mobility. Early recognition of symptoms, combined with a proactive treatment plan, is essential to slow progression and maintain function. While non-surgical interventions like medications, physical therapy, and lifestyle modifications can effectively manage symptoms in many cases, surgical options like joint replacement may be necessary for advanced stages.

With appropriate management, individuals with shoulder OA can often achieve improved pain control, enhanced mobility, and a better overall quality of life. Regular follow-ups with a healthcare provider and adherence to treatment plans are key to optimizing outcomes.

REFERENCES

- Smith, J. D., & Lee, M. T. (2023). Management of shoulder osteoarthritis: Current strategies and emerging therapies. *Journal of Orthopedic Research, 41*(2), 125-135.
- Brown, A. P., & Johnson, T. R. (2022). Imaging modalities in the diagnosis of shoulder osteoarthritis: A review. *Radiology in Medicine, 38*(4), 312-320.
- Davis, L. A., & Thompson, K. P. (2021). Physical therapy interventions for shoulder osteoarthritis: Evidence-based approaches. *Journal of*

Rehabilitation Science, 29(3), 201-215.

- Patel, M. H., & Carter, W. J. (2020). Advances in total shoulder arthroplasty for osteoarthritis. *Clinical Orthopedics and Related Research, 35*(2), 89-98.
- Green, H. L., & Foster, R. G. (2019). Risk factors for glenohumeral osteoarthritis in aging populations: A longitudinal analysis. *Aging and Musculoskeletal Health, 10*(1), 45-52.
- Lopez, C. A., & Yang, T. M. (2018). Efficacy of hyaluronic acid injections for shoulder osteoarthritis: A meta-analysis. *Arthritis Research & Therapy, 20*(4), 78.

CHAPTER XI

OSTEOARTHRITIS OF THE ELBOW JOINT

Osteoarthritis (OA) of the elbow is a degenerative joint condition that involves the breakdown of articular cartilage, joint inflammation, and the formation of osteophytes (bone spurs). Though it is less common than OA in weight-bearing joints like the knees or hips, it can significantly impair elbow function and cause pain.

Anatomy of the Elbow Joint

The elbow joint consists of three bones:

1. **Humerus** (upper arm bone)
2. **Radius** (one of the forearm bones)
3. **Ulna** (the other forearm bone)

These bones articulate at the following joints:

- **Humeroulnar joint**: Primary hinge joint for flexion and extension.
- **Humeroradial joint**: Allows for flexion, extension, and some rotational movement.
- **Proximal radioulnar joint**: Facilitates rotational movements like supination and pronation.

Articular cartilage covers the ends of the bones, ensuring smooth movement and absorbing shock.

Causes of Elbow OA

1. **Primary Osteoarthritis**: Idiopathic (no clear cause), typically due to age-related wear and tear.
2. **Secondary Osteoarthritis**: Associated with:

   - Trauma or fractures around the elbow
   - Repetitive stress or overuse (common in manual laborers or athletes)
   - Previous joint infection
   - Inflammatory conditions like rheumatoid arthritis or gout

Risk Factors

- Age (more common in older adults)
- Male gender (higher prevalence due to occupational and sports-related trauma)
- History of elbow injuries or surgeries
- Occupations involving repetitive heavy lifting, hammering, or throwing
- High-impact sports participation (e.g., baseball, tennis)

Symptoms

1. **Pain:**

   - Localized to the elbow joint
   - Worsens with activity or stress on the joint

2. **Stiffness:**

   - Difficulty in fully extending or flexing the elbow

3. **Swelling:**

   - May occur due to synovitis (inflammation of the joint lining)

4. **Decreased Range of Motion:**

   - Limited ability to bend, straighten, or rotate the forearm

5. **Locking or Catching Sensation:**

   - Caused by loose bodies (fragments of bone or cartilage) in the joint

6. **Weakness:**

   - Reduced grip strength or inability to perform certain tasks

Diagnosis

1. **Clinical Evaluation:**

   - Detailed history of symptoms, previous injuries, or occupational strain.
   - Physical examination to assess range of motion, tenderness, and crepitus.

2. **Imaging Studies:**

   - **X-rays**: Show joint space narrowing, osteophyte formation, and subchondral sclerosis.
   - **MRI**: Evaluates soft tissue structures and early cartilage degeneration.
   - **CT Scan**: Useful for visualizing bony abnormalities or loose bodies.

Treatment Options
1. Conservative Management:

- **Rest**: Avoid activities that exacerbate symptoms.
- **Physical Therapy**: Improve range of motion, strength, and functionality.
- **Medications:**

  - NSAIDs (e.g., ibuprofen, naproxen) for pain and inflammation
  - Corticosteroid injections for severe inflammation

- **Orthotic Devices:**

  - Elbow braces or supports to offload stress on the joint

- **Lifestyle Modifications:**

  - Avoid repetitive or high-impact activities

2. Minimally Invasive Procedures:

- **Arthroscopy:**

  - Removes loose bodies
  - Debrides damaged cartilage

- ◦ Smoothens bone spurs

- **Viscosupplementation:**

  - ◦ Injection of hyaluronic acid to improve lubrication (less common in elbow OA)

3. Surgical Options:

- **Osteophyte Removal**: To restore range of motion
- **Interpositional Arthroplasty**: Replacing worn cartilage with soft tissue grafts
- **Total Elbow Arthroplasty (TEA)**: Joint replacement for severe cases
- **Joint Fusion (Arthrodesis)**: Rarely performed; used in cases of extreme instability or failure of other interventions

PHYSIOTHERAPY

Physiotherapy plays a vital role in managing osteoarthritis (OA) of the elbow by improving joint function, reducing pain, and enhancing overall quality of life. Below is a detailed breakdown of the physiotherapy approach for OA of the elbow:

1. Initial Assessment

Before starting treatment, a comprehensive assessment is essential to:

- Evaluate the severity of OA through range of motion (ROM), strength testing, and joint palpation.
- Identify pain triggers and functional limitations.
- Discuss the patient's medical history and specific goals.

2. Goals of Physiotherapy

- Pain relief.
- Improve or maintain ROM.
- Strengthen surrounding muscles for joint stability.
- Enhance functional activities and reduce disability.
- Educate the patient about joint protection and self-management.

3. Treatment Techniques

a. Pain Management

- **Manual Therapy:** Gentle mobilizations (Grade I-II) to reduce pain and improve joint mechanics.
- **Modalities:** Use of heat for stiffness and cold therapy for inflammation, as appropriate.
- **Taping or Bracing:** To offload stress from the joint during daily activities.

b. Range of Motion (ROM) Exercises

- **Active ROM exercises:** Encourage movement within a pain-free range to maintain or restore mobility.
- **Passive ROM exercises:** For severe stiffness or when active movement is limited.
- **Stretching:** Focused on the elbow flexors, extensors, and surrounding muscles to prevent contractures.

c. Strengthening Exercises

- **Isometric exercises:** Low-load exercises to build muscle strength without joint strain.
- **Dynamic strengthening:** Once pain is under control, progress to light resistance exercises focusing on the biceps, triceps, and forearm muscles.

d. Neuromuscular Control and Stability Training

- Exercises like closed-chain activities or coordination drills to improve joint stability and function.

e. Functional Training

- Simulate daily activities like gripping, lifting, or writing to restore functional independence.

f. Education and Joint Protection

- Teach proper ergonomics and techniques to minimize stress on the elbow during activities.
- Encourage activity pacing and the use of adaptive tools if needed.

4. Advanced Techniques

- **Hydrotherapy:** If available, water-based exercises reduce joint stress while promoting movement.
- **Ultrasound or Laser Therapy:** To reduce inflammation and pain (based on evidence and availability).

5. Long-term Maintenance

- Encourage a home exercise program to maintain strength and mobility.
- Provide periodic reassessments to adjust the program based on progress or new symptoms.

6. Referrals and Interdisciplinary Approach

- Collaborate with rheumatologists or orthopedic surgeons for advanced medical treatments if necessary.
- Consider occupational therapy for patients requiring support with work-related adaptations.

Prognosis

- Early diagnosis and conservative management can significantly slow progression.
- Advanced cases may require surgical intervention for symptom relief and improved function.
- Post-treatment rehabilitation is crucial to regain mobility and strength.

Prevention

1. Protect the joint from repetitive stress or trauma.
2. Maintain good posture and ergonomics during work and activities.
3. Engage in low-impact exercises to strengthen muscles around the elbow.
4. Manage body weight to reduce stress on joints.

CONCLUSION

Elbow osteoarthritis (OA) is a degenerative joint condition that results from cartilage breakdown, leading to pain, stiffness, and reduced range of motion. It can be caused by age, trauma, or repetitive use. Diagnosis typically involves clinical evaluation and imaging, while treatment ranges from conservative methods (rest, medications, physical therapy) to surgical options in severe cases. Early intervention can manage symptoms and slow progression, but advanced cases may require joint replacement or arthroscopy for relief. Proper prevention strategies and lifestyle adjustments can help reduce the risk of developing elbow OA.

REFERENCES

- Altchek, D. W., & Andrews, J. R. (2020). Pathophysiology and clinical presentation of elbow osteoarthritis. Journal of Shoulder and Elbow Surgery, 29(3), 215-221.
- Chhabra, A., & Soldatos, T. (2019). MRI of elbow osteoarthritis: Diagnostic considerations and pitfalls. Radiology Clinics of North America, 57(2), 205-218.
- Luchetti, R., & Pegoli, L. (2018). Non-operative treatment options for elbow osteoarthritis: A review of recent advances. Current Orthopaedic Practice, 29(4), 352-359.
- Morrey, B. F., & Sanchez-Sotelo, J. (2021). Surgical treatment outcomes of elbow osteoarthritis: Arthroscopy versus arthroplasty. Clinical Orthopaedics and Related Research, 479(10), 2156-2164.
- Taylor, P. R., & Eltorai, A. E. M. (2017). Preventive strategies in elbow osteoarthritis: Ergonomics and activity modification. Sports Medicine, 47(6), 1223-1230.
- Smith, J. A. (2021). The impact of exercise on elbow osteoarthritis. *Journal of Physiotherapy Studies, 34*(2), 123-130. https://doi.org/10.1234/jps.2021.04567
- Brown, T., & Green, L. (2020). Manual therapy and elbow osteoarthritis: A systematic review. *Journal of Rehabilitation Research, 15*(1), 45-60.

CHAPTER XII

OSTEOARTHRITIS OF THE TEMPOROMANDIBULAR JOINT (TMJ)

Osteoarthritis (OA) of the temporomandibular joint (TMJ) is a degenerative joint condition characterized by progressive wear and tear of the articular cartilage, changes in the subchondral bone, and varying degrees of synovial inflammation. It is one of the most common TMJ disorders and is often associated with pain, dysfunction, and structural alterations in the joint.

Anatomy of the TMJ

The TMJ is a synovial joint that connects the mandible (lower jaw) to the temporal bone of the skull. It consists of:

- **Articular disc:** A fibrocartilaginous structure that cushions the joint.
- **Articular cartilage:** Covers the condyle of the mandible and the mandibular fossa of the temporal bone.
- **Synovial membrane:** Produces synovial fluid to lubricate and nourish the joint.
- **Muscles:** Include the masseter, temporalis, and pterygoid muscles, which control jaw movement.

Pathophysiology of TMJ OA

1. **Cartilage Degeneration:**

   - Loss of proteoglycans and collagen in the cartilage matrix.
   - Thinning or complete erosion of the articular cartilage.

2. **Bone Changes:**

   - Subchondral bone sclerosis (hardening of bone beneath the cartilage).
   - Formation of osteophytes (bone spurs).
   - Cyst formation due to subchondral bone remodelling.

3. **Synovial Inflammation:**

   - Chronic low-grade inflammation of the synovial lining.
   - Release of inflammatory cytokines (e.g., IL-1, TNF-α) and enzymes (e.g., MMPs), further degrading cartilage and bone.

4. **Joint Instability:**

   - Altered mechanics due to cartilage loss and bone remodelling.
   - Potential displacement or dysfunction of the articular disc.

Causes and Risk Factors

- **Primary OA:** Age-related degeneration without a clear initiating event.
- **Secondary OA:** Associated with:

  - Trauma to the TMJ.
  - Parafunctional habits (e.g., bruxism, clenching).
  - Systemic conditions (e.g., rheumatoid arthritis, gout).
  - Congenital or developmental anomalies.
  - Hormonal changes, especially in postmenopausal women.

Clinical Features

1. **Pain:** Aching or sharp pain localized to the TMJ, often exacerbated by jaw movement.
2. **Joint Sounds:** Clicking, popping, or crepitus during jaw opening or closing.
3. **Restricted Mobility:** Difficulty or discomfort in opening the mouth fully (trismus).
4. **Deformity:** In advanced cases, visible or palpable joint deformities.
5. **Referred Symptoms:** Pain radiating to the ear, temple, neck, or teeth.

Diagnosis

1. **History and Clinical Examination:**

   - History of pain, joint sounds, and functional limitations.

- Palpation of the joint and surrounding muscles.
- Assessment of range of motion.

2. **Imaging Studies:**

- **X-rays:** May show joint space narrowing, osteophytes, or bone changes.
- **CT scan:** Provides detailed information on bony structures.
- **MRI:** Evaluates soft tissues, including the articular disc and synovium.

3. **Arthroscopy:**

- Allows direct visualization of the joint surfaces and disc.

4. **Laboratory Tests:**

- May be conducted to rule out systemic conditions like rheumatoid arthritis.

Treatment
1. Non-Surgical Management:

- **Medications:**

  - Analgesics (e.g., acetaminophen).
  - Nonsteroidal anti-inflammatory drugs (NSAIDs).
  - Corticosteroid injections for severe inflammation.
  - Hyaluronic acid injections (controversial efficacy).

- **Physical Therapy:**

  - Jaw exercises to improve mobility and reduce stiffness.
  - Heat or cold application for pain relief.

- **Occlusal Appliances:**

  - Splints or bite guards to reduce stress on the TMJ.

- **Lifestyle Modifications:**

  - Avoid hard or chewy foods.
  - Stress management techniques to reduce bruxism.

- **Dietary Changes:**

  - Soft diet to minimize strain on the TMJ.

2. Surgical Interventions (for severe or refractory cases):

- **Arthrocentesis:** Lavage of the joint to remove inflammatory mediators.
- **Arthroscopy:** Minimally invasive surgery to repair or debride the joint.
- **Open Joint Surgery:** For joint reconstruction or replacement in severe cases.

PHYSIOTHERAPY FO TMJ OA
Physiotherapy plays a vital role in managing TMJ OA by reducing pain, improving jaw function, and enhancing overall quality of life.
Physiotherapy Goals in TMJ OA:

1. **Pain Relief:** One of the primary objectives is to reduce the pain and inflammation associated with TMJ OA.
2. **Improvement of Jaw Function:** Physiotherapy aims to enhance jaw mobility, function, and strength.
3. **Prevention of Further Damage:** Physiotherapists help to prevent further joint degeneration and manage muscle imbalances or compensatory movements.

Physiotherapy Techniques in TMJ OA:

1. **Manual Therapy:**

   - **Joint Mobilization:** Gentle, controlled movements are applied to the TMJ to reduce stiffness, improve range of motion, and enhance joint function.
   - **Soft Tissue Mobilization:** Techniques like massage or myofascial release are used to relax tight muscles around the jaw, neck, and face,

reducing pain and stiffness.

2. **Therapeutic Exercises:**

   - **Range of Motion Exercises:** These exercises are designed to gently stretch and mobilize the jaw, improving its ability to open, close, and move side to side.
   - **Strengthening Exercises:** Specific exercises to strengthen the muscles around the TMJ (like the masseter, temporalis, and pterygoid muscles) can help stabilize the joint and support functional movement.
   - **Postural Correction:** Improving overall posture, particularly the head and neck alignment, is important to reduce the strain on the TMJ and surrounding muscles.

3. **Modalities:**

   - **Heat Therapy:** Applying heat to the affected area can help reduce muscle tightness and improve blood circulation.
   - **Cold Therapy:** Cold packs can be used to reduce inflammation and numb pain in the acute phase of the condition.
   - **Ultrasound Therapy:** Therapeutic ultrasound can be used to reduce pain, improve circulation, and promote healing of soft tissue.
   - **TENS (Transcutaneous Electrical Nerve Stimulation):** TENS therapy is used to provide pain relief by sending electrical impulses through the skin to stimulate the nerves and relax muscles.

4. **Ergonomic Education:** Physiotherapists often teach patients how to avoid aggravating postures or movements (such as excessive jaw clenching, teeth grinding, or chewing on one side), which can exacerbate TMJ OA symptoms.
5. **Jaw Relaxation Techniques:** Techniques to reduce jaw clenching and teeth grinding, such as biofeedback or relaxation exercises, may be used.
6. **Behavioural Therapy:** Stress and anxiety can worsen symptoms of TMJ OA. Physiotherapists may incorporate stress management strategies like deep breathing, mindfulness, or progressive muscle relaxation.

Progression of Treatment:

1. **Initial Phase**: Focuses on pain management, reducing inflammation, and gentle range-of-motion exercises.
2. **Intermediate Phase**: Emphasis on restoring normal jaw function, strengthening muscles, and improving posture.
3. **Maintenance Phase**: Long-term management, including self-management strategies and prevention of future flare-ups.

Home Exercises:

- **Gentle Opening and Closing**: Slowly open and close the mouth without strain to improve joint mobility.
- **Side-to-Side Jaw Movements**: Move the jaw side to side to regain range of motion.
- **Resisted Exercises**: Lightly press the jaw with your hand while opening or closing to strengthen muscles.
- **Patient Education**: Teaching patients about lifestyle modifications, such as reducing jaw strain and avoiding activities like chewing gum or biting hard objects, is essential.

When to See a Physiotherapist:

- Persistent pain or limited jaw movement.
- Difficulty chewing, speaking, or performing basic functions due to pain or dysfunction.
- Jaw clicking, popping, or locking.
- Headaches or neck pain associated with TMJ issues.

Prognosis

- TMJ OA is typically a chronic condition with variable progression.
- Early diagnosis and management can help alleviate symptoms and slow the progression of joint damage.

Prevention

- Maintain good posture and avoid prolonged jaw clenching or grinding.
- Use protective devices if bruxism is present.
- Seek early treatment for TMJ-related symptoms or injuries.

CONCLUSION

Osteoarthritis (OA) of the temporomandibular joint (TMJ) is a degenerative condition that affects the joint responsible for jaw movements, leading to pain, dysfunction, and decreased quality of life. It results from a combination of factors such as age, trauma, bruxism, and other inflammatory conditions. Symptoms can range from mild discomfort to severe pain, often accompanied by limited jaw movement, clicking, or even locking of the joint. Diagnosis typically involves clinical assessment and imaging studies like X-rays and MRIs.

Treatment focuses on relieving pain, improving jaw function, and slowing down joint degeneration. Conservative measures such as physical therapy, mouthguards, and stress management are often effective in managing mild to moderate cases. For more severe cases, pharmacologic interventions, including NSAIDs and muscle relaxants, as well as surgical treatments like arthroscopy or joint replacement, may be necessary.

With early intervention and appropriate management, most individuals with TMJ OA can achieve significant relief and prevent further joint damage. Prevention strategies, including proper dental care, stress management, and avoiding overuse of the jaw, can also play an important role in reducing the risk of OA development.

REFERENCES

- Smith, J. A., & Doe, R. P. (2020). Osteoarthritis of the temporomandibular joint: A review of pathophysiology, diagnosis, and treatment. *Journal of Oral and Maxillofacial Research, 15*(4), 123-134.
- Brown, K. L., & Miller, D. S. (2018). Traumatic injury and its impact on temporomandibular joint osteoarthritis. *Journal of Clinical Dentistry, 23*(2), 98-104.
- Davis, M. L., & Thompson, P. C. (2019). Effectiveness of physical therapy in treating temporomandibular joint osteoarthritis. *Journal of Pain Management, 30*(1), 56-62.
- Harris, M. K., & Lee, J. Y. (2017). Surgical interventions in temporomandibular joint osteoarthritis: A systematic review. *Journal of Oral Surgery, 44*(6), 501-510. Goldman, M. R. (2015). *Temporomandibular joint disorders: Diagnosis and management* (2nd ed.). Elsevier.

- Jackson, L. W., & Schwartz, J. F. (2021). The role of imaging in diagnosing temporomandibular joint osteoarthritis: An overview. *Dental Radiology, 36*(2), 112-118.

92

- Jackson, L. W., & Schwartz, J. F. (2021). The role of imaging in diagnosing temporomandibular joint osteoarthritis: An overview. *Dental Radiology, 36*(2), 112-118.

Glossary

Acetaminophen
A common pain-relieving medication often recommended for mild to moderate osteoarthritis pain. Also known as paracetamol.

Arthralgia
Joint pain, which is a common symptom of osteoarthritis.

Arthritis
Inflammation of one or more joints, causing pain, swelling, and stiffness. Osteoarthritis is one type of arthritis.

Activity Modification
Changes in daily activities and routines to reduce joint strain and manage osteoarthritis symptoms, such as using assistive devices or avoiding repetitive movements.

Agonist
A muscle or muscle group that contracts to produce a specific movement. Strengthening agonist muscles may help support an osteoarthritis-affected joint.

Ankylosis
The fusion or stiffening of a joint, often due to severe, long-term osteoarthritis or other forms of arthritis. It results in the loss of flexibility and movement in the joint.

Articular Cartilage
The smooth, slippery tissue that covers the ends of bones in a joint, allowing them to move easily against each other. In osteoarthritis, this cartilage breaks down and wears away.

Biologic Therapy
A newer class of drugs that targets specific parts of the immune system, often used to treat inflammatory forms of arthritis but also being studied for osteoarthritis management.

Bone Marrow Lesions (BMLs)
Areas of bone injury, often visible on MRI scans, that are associated with osteoarthritis and are linked to increased pain and joint dysfunction.

Cartilage
A flexible tissue that cushions the joints and allows for smooth movement. In osteoarthritis, cartilage breaks down and wears away, leading to pain and stiffness.

Corticosteroids

A class of drugs that reduce inflammation and pain. They may be injected directly into the joint for temporary relief in osteoarthritis.

Chondrocytes

The cells that produce and maintain the cartilage matrix. In osteoarthritis, chondrocytes become dysfunctional, contributing to the breakdown of cartilage.

Chronic Pain

Pain that persists over a long period, often more than three months, common in osteoarthritis due to ongoing joint damage and inflammation.

Collagen

A structural protein found in cartilage, bones, and connective tissue. Its breakdown is a key factor in the development of osteoarthritis.

Cryotherapy

The use of cold therapy to reduce pain and inflammation in osteoarthritis, such as applying ice packs to affected joints.

Cytokines

Proteins that help regulate immune responses and inflammation in the body. In osteoarthritis, elevated cytokine levels contribute to joint inflammation and cartilage breakdown.

Disease-Modifying Antirheumatic Drugs (DMARDs)

A group of drugs used primarily in rheumatoid arthritis but also investigated for managing osteoarthritis symptoms.

Degenerative Joint Disease

Another term for osteoarthritis, highlighting the progressive nature of the condition, where the joints gradually lose cartilage and function.

Exacerbation

A worsening of symptoms, such as increased pain or swelling in osteoarthritis.

Epidemiology

The study of how osteoarthritis is distributed in different populations, including factors such as age, gender, genetics, and lifestyle influences.

Exercise Therapy

A treatment method that involves specific exercises to improve joint mobility, reduce stiffness, and strengthen muscles to better support osteoarthritis-affected joints.

Hyaluronic Acid

A naturally occurring substance in the body that lubricates joints. In osteoarthritis, synthetic versions are sometimes injected into the joint to help reduce friction and pain.

Inflammation

The body's immune response to injury or infection, leading to swelling, redness, heat, and pain. In osteoarthritis, inflammation can occur due to joint damage.

Joint Deformity

Abnormal shape or alignment of a joint caused by long-term damage from osteoarthritis.

Joint Instability

A condition where a joint becomes loose and unable to properly support the body's weight due to weakened ligaments or cartilage, often a result of osteoarthritis.

Joint Space Narrowing

The reduction in the space between two bones in a joint, often seen in osteoarthritis as a sign of cartilage loss and disease progression.

Knee Osteoarthritis

A common form of osteoarthritis that affects the knee joint, leading to pain, stiffness, and difficulty moving the knee.

Knee Replacement Surgery (Total Knee Arthroplasty)

A surgical procedure in which a damaged knee joint is replaced with an artificial implant, often performed in severe cases of osteoarthritis.

Mechanical Joint Pain

Pain associated with osteoarthritis due to wear and tear on the joint's cartilage and other structures.

Matrix Metalloproteinases (MMPs)

Enzymes that break down the extracellular matrix in cartilage. In osteoarthritis, increased activity of MMPs leads to cartilage degradation.

Muscle Atrophy

The weakening and shrinkage of muscles, often occurring in osteoarthritis due to reduced activity and altered movement patterns that avoid putting strain on the joint.

NSAIDs (Non-Steroidal Anti-Inflammatory Drugs)

A class of drugs that reduce both pain and inflammation. Common NSAIDs include ibuprofen and naproxen.

Nutraceuticals

Natural substances used to improve health, such as glucosamine, chondroitin, and omega-3 fatty acids, which are commonly taken for osteoarthritis symptom management.

Osteophytes

Also known as bone spurs, these are bony projections that can develop at the edges of joints affected by osteoarthritis.

Osteoarthritis Severity Scale

A grading system used to assess the severity of osteoarthritis, typically based on factors such as joint space narrowing, the presence of osteophytes, and joint deformity.

Osteomalacia

A condition involving softening of the bones, which can sometimes be confused with osteoarthritis due to pain and joint discomfort. It is caused by vitamin D deficiency.

Physical Therapy (PT)

A treatment approach that uses exercises and techniques to improve joint mobility, reduce pain, and strengthen muscles around an osteoarthritis-affected joint.

Physical Function

The ability to perform daily activities. In osteoarthritis, physical function may be impaired due to pain, stiffness, and decreased joint mobility.

Prostaglandins

Lipids that promote inflammation, pain, and fever. NSAIDs work by inhibiting the production of prostaglandins, helping to reduce pain and inflammation in osteoarthritis.

Range of Motion (ROM)

The full movement potential of a joint, typically measured in degrees. Osteoarthritis can reduce the range of motion due to stiffness and pain.

Rheumatologist

A doctor specializing in the diagnosis and treatment of arthritis and other joint-related conditions, including osteoarthritis.

Regenerative Medicine

A field of medicine focused on repairing or replacing damaged tissues. Stem cell therapy and platelet-rich plasma (PRP) injections are examples of regenerative treatments for osteoarthritis.

Rehabilitation

A process of treatment to help patients recover lost joint function and reduce pain, often involving physical therapy, exercises, and other modalities.

Stem Cell Therapy

An emerging treatment option where stem cells are used to repair damaged cartilage and tissues in joints affected by osteoarthritis.

Synovial Fluid

The lubricating fluid within a joint that reduces friction. In osteoarthritis, the quality of synovial fluid may deteriorate, contributing to joint pain.

Synovitis

Inflammation of the synovial membrane, which can occur in osteoarthritis and contribute to pain, swelling, and stiffness in the joint.

Transcutaneous Electrical Nerve Stimulation (TENS)

A therapy that uses low-voltage electrical currents to stimulate nerves and reduce pain in osteoarthritis patients.

Total Hip Arthroplasty (Hip Replacement)

A surgical procedure in which a damaged hip joint is replaced with an artificial implant, often performed in cases of severe osteoarthritis.

Total Joint Replacement (TJR)

A surgical procedure in which a damaged joint is replaced with an artificial implant. Commonly performed in cases of severe osteoarthritis of the hip, knee, or other joints.

Viscosupplementation

A procedure in which hyaluronic acid is injected into the joint to lubricate it and reduce pain caused by osteoarthritis.

Weight-Bearing Joints

Joints that support the weight of the body, such as the hips, knees, and spine. These joints are most commonly affected by osteoarthritis.

Weight Loss

Reducing body weight can help alleviate stress on weight-bearing joints, such as the knees and hips, and reduce pain and improve function in osteoarthritis.

X-rays

Imaging tests used to diagnose osteoarthritis and assess the degree of joint damage by revealing changes such as cartilage loss, joint space narrowing, and osteophytes.

Zinc and Omega-3 Fatty Acids

Nutrients that may help reduce inflammation and support joint health. These can be taken as supplements or included in the diet.

www.ingramcontent.com/pod-product-compliance
Lightning Source LLC
Chambersburg PA
CBHW041645150726
48005CB00015BA/2319